MOM, I NEED TO BE A GIRL,
Second Edition

by
Just Evelyn

Illustrated by Andrew Warhmund

i

Mom, I Need to be a Girl, Second Edition

ISBN-10: 1-4196-8438-8
ISBN-13: 9781419684388

Published by Just Evelyn, Longmont, CO.
Illustrations Copyright © 1998 Andrew Wahrmund

First Edition, Copyright © 1998 Just Evelyn.

Second Edition Editing: Kelley Winters and Lacey Lawrence
First Edition Editing: Dawn Trook
Cover Idea: Julia Kate Morgan
Cover Illustration: Andrew Wahrmund
Rear Cover text and Glossary definitions used with permission,
TransYouth Family Advocates, Inc.

Some names have been changed to protect the innocent and the incompetent.

DEDICATION

This book is dedicated to my new daughter, who has taught me so much about being brave and true to oneself; and also to the memory of Ian Benson, Tenie, and Julia.

ACKNOWLEDGEMENTS

I want to thank all those who helped make this book possible. Thanks to my mother, Clela Fuller Morgan, who did much of the typing and organizing of the stories. Thanks to all my children for making my life interesting. Thanks to the Writing Center. Thanks to my friends who listened and encouraged me: Tom, Lorne, Susan, Caroline, Walter, Dawn, Kelly, Karry, Serena, Hallie, Elena, Janine, Dave, Andrew, Jenna, Joyce, Brent, Michelle, Nicole and too many others to name.

I also want to thank those special people who stood by Danielle and helped her through this new part of her life: My sister, Denise, Laura, Miguel, Gloria, Diane, Danica, Joe, Joni and the members of the New Images cast.

2nd Edition Acknowledgements

In my travels with the gender diverse communities in the last 15 years, I have learned so much from so many interesting people. I would love to thank each and every one for their stories about their lives that they have shared with me. It is hard to thank just a few, but in the interest of time and space I would like to add a few names: Lacey Lawrence, who keeps me sane and enjoying life and helped edit this edition; Karla, who has become a big part of my family; Kelley Winters, who did the technical aspects that overwhelm me and helped with good advice; Aunty Jen, who has been there for so many gender variant teens and all those who encouraged me to put this book back in print.

Thanks to Lynn Conway, who has maintained the book on her website for these many years, for all her efforts and to those volunteers who have translated this book into different languages on Lynn's website. Even though the first printing sold out in a few years, it has continued to spread with the help of many volunteers and web sites. This book has found its way into many foreign countries, and I wish I could have been a mouse in the corner to see the circumstances surrounding its arrival. I have always hoped that it helped other brave teens find their way, or helped other parents get through transition time with hope to eventually celebrate their beautiful children. I have joined a dedicated group of parents and allies called TYFA (TransYouth Family Advocates). I am donating the profits from this 2nd Edition to continue the work among gender variant youth.

CONTENTS

INTRODUCTION

You are about to read a rare true story about a young boy who received a kind of help from his mother that some children need, but almost none receive.

Daniel should have been born a girl. In these pages, you will meet Daniel's father who believes that sexual reassignment is against God. You'll follow the fencing matches with bureaucrats, and the contest of wills with councilors whose skills are so often limited to dream-obstruction and fee collection. Most importantly, you'll read how Daniel's courageous and superbly understanding mother helped Daniel to become the charming, irrepressible Danielle, despite a globe full of minor tyrants, tunnel vision functionaries, buffoons, financial opportunists, and misguided do-gooders trying to prevent it.

I have finally met Danielle now 19, after having heard and been entertained by her exploits every week for months during my electrolysis sessions with her mother. I am deeply impressed. Danielle's fitness for life as a teenage girl and success at it, as well as her happiness and maturity bring glad, wistful tears to my much older eyes--wistful, because I, too, am a transsexual.

I lived through Danielle's childhood experiences of having the wrong body, but because I grew up in the 50's and 60's, and because of the less communicative, sexually repressed atmosphere of my family, I had to go through full male puberty, attend male gym classes, deal with bullies, and miss out on many years of shopping and dating. I hit every stump, bramble bush and pothole that waits for us folk who hack our way along the wrong road of life.

But it's 1998 now, and things are changing. Danielle's experience is one of the first in what promises to be a new and better era for people like her and like me.

Hallie Horowitz

Something to tell you mom . . .

PART I.........ANGUISH

"I need to talk to you Mom. I have something to tell you, but I'm afraid you won't love me any more." My fifteen-year-old son lay down beside me on the bed in our usual family conference tradition. The children knew they had my undivided attention when I was already in bed.

I assured him that no matter what he told me, I would still love him. He hemmed and hawed and I thought he might be going to tell me he was gay. I had suspected that he was gay for years and had hoped such a conversation would take place sometime so that we could get involved in the gay community support system. However, he had something entirely different on his mind.

He said, "I need to be a girl. I'm a girl inside. I like boys but as a woman would, not the gay way. I have felt this way for years, and you know how feminine I am."

So this was what he had been upset about the last few months. At first I didn't know what to say. I hugged him and thought, "Oprah Winfrey, where are you?" I rarely watched television, and daytime talk shows even less, so I had not been exposed to this issue before. Everything seemed to move in slow motion. I felt my life was taking a definite turn; I knew it would never be the same again.

After a long silence he asked, "What are we going to do?"

"I honestly don't know what to do, but I'll find out," I answered.

After we laughed and cried together I asked, "Have you ever worn my clothes?"

His response was, "I would never wear your funky old clothes," and I believed him. Besides being bigger than him, I knew he did not approve of my non-fashions. He scolded me for my lack of interest in fashion or make up or hairstyles. He said, "You are a woman and can do all those things, and yet you don't. That's such a waste!"

We talked about his childhood. He admitted trying on his female cousin's clothes. He was happy when someone mistook him for a girl because of his feminine appearance although I had always assured him he looked otherwise. He always felt bad when I talked about how proud I was of my three sons. I had often added, "I'm glad I don't have any girls, because they're harder to raise." Sometimes I said, "The world is not yet ready for any girl I would have raised," Because I would have encouraged a girl to join little league or be a jet fighter pilot or president. How prophetic that turned out to be as I am now raising a girl that the world is not ready for. I had always told my children that they could be anything that they wanted to be when they grew up, but I never dreamed that one of my boys would want to grow up to be a woman.

"I just want to be normal, and normal is being a girl. I'm tired of not being myself I'm tired of being confused. I just want to be a girl. I have no future as a man. I wanted to run away from home so that I could be a girl where no one knew me, but I knew it would hurt you." I asked him if he wanted to move to a new school and go as a girl the next year. "I can muddle through high-school as a boy," he replied, "I don't think going to school as a girl will be a solution because I would just be hiding and pretending from another side." He wanted to BE a girl, not just dress-up as a girl.

He finally fell asleep beside me. Meanwhile, my mind was wide awake forming dozens of questions. What happens to these kids? Is this just a phase? Is this part of being gay? If I don't make a big deal about it, will it just go away? Is there a name for this condition? Does this usually happen to people so young, and can they change? Can they succeed in life? I wanted information and I wanted it now, in the middle of the night!

What does a mother do in this situation? When my boys came to me with a cut, I would put on a Band-Aid and a kiss to make it better, but I had no Band-Aids for this problem. I knew his life would be difficult and sad. How could a mother help, and would a mother's love be enough? Was I strong enough to handle this? I thought I knew my boys pretty well, yet I had no idea that Daniel's life was so troubled.

* * * * *

This was the beginning of just one more chapter in my unconventional life. I spent some of my childhood in Africa with my missionary parents, so I had been exposed to travel, adventure, and attempts to change the world. I was also the anti-establishment, back-to-nature type and had dropped out of college to volunteer my time and talents to a school in a small Mexican village. There I met Salvador, a man with beautiful Latin eyes, a man whose world was limited to a town so small it had only one paved road. His simple, self-sufficient life style seemed attractive to me. We grew our own food, owned a cow, and I made our clothes.

We lived in an old adobe house without water or electricity. After our first son David was born, we moved to California, the first of several moves between Mexico and the States. After Benjamin and Daniel were born in California, we moved back to Mexico into a new, modern home that we spent several years building. A few months later we were hit by a flash flood during extraordinarily heavy spring rains. The children and I were marooned for several hours on the top bunk bed while we watched the furniture float out the double doors and down the river. Fortunately we were rescued before the whole house washed away.

For ten years I tried to prove to everyone that I could make this marriage work, but reality finally set in when I became resentful of Salvador's attempt to isolate us even from his own family. I finally decided to leave, taking the boys, ages three, five and nine, with me.

Their father said, "Since you are leaving and taking the kids, I expect you to be able to support them. If you want any help, you can come back and live with me." Salvador lived up to his word and never provided any support, and I never returned to him nor asked for his financial help.

Life was not easy as a single mother receiving no child support. I was in a constant panic about money, always hoping the end of the month would arrive before the end of the money. We lived sometimes in the city, sometimes in the country with a variety of pets - a destructive dog, a bird, fish and a horse. There were paper routes, music lessons, and summer camps.

After four years on welfare, I started working full time as a file clerk in a hospital and Daniel started school.

I worked a second job, which made it possible to keep a roof over our head and food on the table. However, it didn't allow me much time to be with the boys. They learned to take care of themselves and each other. There was always a fear in the back of my mind that the Child Protective Agency or other authorities would discover the boys at home alone and take them away. It almost happened when police came in response to a frivolous 911 call placed from our house by a neighbor girl. They found 12-year old Ben, and 10-year old Daniel alone. The law allowed a 12-year old to be alone, but not baby-sitting a younger child. Ben and Daniel offered the officers peanut butter sandwiches, and asked them for help with a computer game. The police concluded that they were well fed and were good kids. They left with the admonition that their mother find someone to watch them during the times when they had to be alone because of David's schedule.

David became my dependable helper and baby-sitter for his younger brothers - he even took a Red Cross baby-sitting course. My children were quite self-sufficient, for they had learned to grocery shop, feed themselves, wash clothes and handle money. I could give them $20 when that was all I had for food until the end of the week, and they would decide which necessities to buy. Ben could estimate the total amount of their purchases within pennies, so they would not be embarrassed at the checkout stand. They helped me write cheeks and balance my bank account. They understood that they needed to help me by staying out of trouble. I didn't want them to worry, but I needed the help and I believed in accepting reality.

We moved quite often because I had to live where I found work, or there was trouble with neighbors or housemates or the local school, or the apartment owner raised the rent. We even moved temporarily to the east coast, traveling both there and back by Greyhound Bus. We were a team so my children always helped with the decisions about moving. I didn't make any rules because I wasn't home to enforce them. I raised them using the theory that I expected them to be good, and they were. I let them learn from their mistakes. If they stayed up too late, it was hard to get up for work or school the next day. They set their own alarm clocks because I was often off to work before they were up.

My children were brought up without God even though I had no idea how to raise children without religion. I was raised in a conservative Christian home where sin, punishment and guilt seemed to be waiting around every corner. It is my belief that I am responsible for my actions. If there is a God, He does not need my adoration or my money. I don't believe that He is involved in the day-to-day happenings of every person's life. I did like to think there was a strong feminine force up there somewhere watching over my children when they were out of my sight, a heavenly grandmother.

David's great sense of humor and responsibility helped me to keep things in perspective. At sixteen he got his driver's license and my mother gave him a used car. I sat down with him and said, "Now that Grandma Clela has given you a car, we need to make rules about driving."

He asked, "Why?"

After thinking about it, I could come up with no reason that made sense since he had always demonstrated exceptional maturity. So together we decided no rules would be necessary as long as he was responsible and kept out of trouble. And there were never any problems. He would often come home from a date or school activity, wake me up and sit on the bed beside me while telling me all about his evening. Even when I was very tired, I was glad he wanted to talk to me because I loved being involved in his life.

Ben, who is four years younger than David, and very bright, was not being challenged in school, even in the classes for gifted students. He had a keen interest in money and showed signs of being an entrepreneur at an early age. He sometimes offered to clean out my purse for the loose change, or clip coupons for items that we regularly used, and I was glad to give him the savings. When we had a garage sale, it was Ben that priced the items and handled the money. In third grade he chose the baritone horn and played in the band. The horn was almost as big as he was, but he trudged off to school every day hauling it behind him on a trash can carrier. He became very proficient as he played that huge horn through high school while learning other brass instruments as well. He easily picked up computer skills, and was a good athlete excelling in anything he tried. As the middle child only two years older than Daniel, I probably neglected him somewhat, but he did well on his own.

Then there was Daniel! He was a loving and cuddly child, but he was a handful! He didn't hit his terrible two's until he was five, and then I thought he would never get over them. He always tested me to the limit. If I said, "No," to touching one trinket on a shelf, he tried each one to see if I would say "No."

Brushing and arranging my long, curly hair was a favorite pastime for Daniel when he was about three years old. During his early teen years he could arrange my thick curls into a spectacular hairdo for a special occasion. He was very fashion conscious and always aware of the current styles. He most often chose unisex styles for himself in bright colors, and then washed them by hand so they would not fade. When I went shopping for clothes for myself, he enjoyed going along to advise me. In retrospect, I think he was living vicariously through me because he could not wear feminine fashions himself.

Ben and David tried unsuccessfully to get Daniel involved in some of the more rough-and-tumble games. However, he became quite skilled in the art of self-defense when his brothers teased or made fun of him. Once I came home to find the two older boys in a corner while Daniel wielded a broomstick that he used very effectively if they tried to escape.

Most sports held no interest for Daniel, but he enjoyed roller skating and took classes in tap dancing and gymnastics. Because he had few successes in school, I encouraged him in these other interests to boost his self-confidence. He was especially talented in gymnastics, and his brothers heaped praise on him when he did hand stands, one-handed somersaults, and other tricks beyond what they were able to do.

Daniel always preferred playing with girls rather than boys. In the toy box at Grandma Clela's house, the old doll was his favorite. Daniel liked to sew, cook, and clean house. Since I spent little time on these traditional female activities, he was not following my example. He rearranged the furniture to his taste, and looked for pictures and other items to decorate the walls.

After much hard work, I started my own business doing cancer statistics. Self-employment fit my personality because I like to control my own life. It also allowed me to have a flexible work schedule. The pay was adequate so that we no longer had to count pennies, and we were able to get out of debt. I was proud that I was the breadwinner; I was providing for my family, and doing it better than many families with two parents. Women in our society seldom have such an opportunity. Many single mothers I knew were playing the role of victim, dependent on the whim of the father to provide child support. For many years I dreamed of someone to share the responsibility and the joys of watching my children grow up. However, most of the men with whom I formed relationships added to my responsibilities, and did not enjoy the boys as much as I had hoped. Being single suited me fine, for the boys were the focus of my attention and concern.

As Daniel finished the eighth grade, I saw signs of increasing tension. He seemed to enjoy school and socializing with the other students, but something was bothering him. He was not able to fall asleep at night, and when he did, he did not sleep well. He knew he had to get some sleep to feel well for school the next day, so we tried warm milk, watched boring television, sang lullabies, told stories, and did the mental exercise "walking through a dark friendly forest, you are getting tired." We also talked about a great variety of topics.

Once he said, "I don't know who I am."

I responded, "Most teenagers feel that way. Most of the kids at your school probably feel the same way."

"When my teen years are over, I won't feel this way anymore?" he asked.

"That's right. You just have to get through your teen years." Little did I know just how difficult getting through those next few years was going to be for him.

I don't know who I am.

* * * * *

During Ben's sophomore year in high school, he went to live with David, who was attending college in Phoenix. It wasn't easy to let Ben leave home when he was still young, but it solved several problems. Daniel, Ben and I were living in the country: an hour's bus ride from the nearest high school. My work schedule prevented me from driving him to and from school so he felt pretty isolated. He was unhappy because the transportation problem kept him from participating in after-school band or sports activities. David was living in an apartment but had trouble finding responsible roommates. David suggested that Ben could live with him and attend the nearby high school.

I was sad to have Ben leave and a little apprehensive about the arrangement, but they wanted to try it. Besides he could always come home if it didn't work out well. I paid Ben's share of the apartment rent, but otherwise they were mostly supporting themselves. David and Ben had a credit card on my account to be used when they needed money unexpectedly. They never used it without telling me, and never used it unwisely. I was proud of them as they responsibly went to school, worked, paid their bills, and kept track of each other.

Whenever possible I've allowed my children to shape their own lives, and tried not to curb their adventurous endeavors because of my anxiety. I was proud of David and Ben as they proved to me that they understood the meaning of responsibility. My friends were amazed at this unusual arrangement. Parents are often unable to manage their teenagers living at home let alone trust a couple of brothers to take complete control of their lives 400 miles away from any family.

With my child-rearing days were almost over, there was light at the end of the tunnel. I just didn't realize how long the tunnel was.

After his revelation, Daniel was peaceful and calm, but I was a basket case. I tried to maintain an outward appearance of composure, but my mind would not work well due to stress and lack of sleep.

The next morning Daniel spent hours in front of the mirror in my room. He styled his hair, put on make-up, shaved his legs, and created short-shorts from a pair of long pants. When he tied a T-shirt up tight above his waist, he did look like a girl. It was amazing to watch the transformation. However, he still adopted the unisex look in front of others, and he did not want me to tell his brothers yet.

When we went shopping later that day, Daniel said he needed underwear, and I wondered whether he was thinking about panties. I didn't ask, but just told him to get what he needed because I wanted to avoid the whole subject. He chose his usual jockey shorts, and I breathed a sigh of relief. I kept watching for signs of something - I'm not sure what.

I asked one of my friends to meet me at the mall because I really need to talk to someone. He hazarded several guesses as to the cause of my problem, but I knew he would never guess. When my friend learned the cause of my dismay, he agreed he never would have guessed. He thought the condition was called gender dysphoria or transsexualism. He advised me to research the subject at the medical library of our local university hospital.

Another friend who knew my children well expressed his support but did not know much about gender problems either. However, a few days later he called with some troubling information. A gay friend of his had told him that transsexuals have an even a harder life than gays for they are at the far end of the spectrum when it comes to acceptance in the community. He also expressed sympathy for us because he knew we had a hard road ahead and suggested that I go to the Gay and Lesbian Center to seek information.

Daniel had gone to visit his brothers as soon as school was out. Ben brought him back and was visiting from Arizona for the Fourth of July holidays. I was close to tears all day. Contrary to Daniel's wishes, I told Ben the reason for my distress because I needed to share it with someone. Ben said, "It's no big deal. Daniel probably just needs more attention." When Ben was ready to return to Phoenix, Daniel wanted to go back with him. He wanted to be able to go out shopping at the mall as a girl without the fear of running into his friends. David and Ben approved the plan as they liked to have him cook and keep their apartment clean while they worked or attended school. Daniel had played with several feminine names, such as Jasmine or Danny, but seemed to be settling on Danielle.

My instincts told me that momentous events would take place during Danielle's second visit to Arizona, and I talked to my children there almost every day so as to be a part of it.

Danielle told me about Denise, who was a good friend and neighbor to Ben and David. Denise had known a transsexual, and recognized the signs in Danielle, so she took her under her wing. While the older boys were away, she and Danielle experimented with hair and make-up, and did all the things that girlfriends do - the things that Danielle had always longed to do. Danielle confessed she took some of my make-up with her - make-up that she encouraged me to buy a year before when she saw it on television. I didn't mind because I seldom used it. Danielle kept me informed about all the new things she was doing, and told me everything she bought during her mall trips with Denise. David used my credit card to get cash advances for Danielle's use, and she told me how much she paid for each item because she was concerned about my having to spend money on her.

It was Denise who told David about transsexuals and what was happening to Danielle. When David told me he knew, I cried with gratitude for Denise. Bless her dear, dear spirit - I just wanted to hug her. David was quite stressed by all the new developments. He was doing his best to hide his feelings from Danielle - he began to work out at the gym more than usual. Ben persisted in his opinion that Danielle just needed more attention. He bought her a computer art program and was trying to teach her how to use it. It was clever of Ben to find a way to give her more attention that involved his beloved computer.

Danielle told me her brothers were treating her nicely, and she thought they were glad to find out that she was not gay. She told me she saw an 18-year old transsexual on a television talk show and said, "I think I could have done better at expressing how it feels inside."

Denise thought Danielle was passing very well as a girl - the guys were even checking her out at the malls. Denise had to remind Danielle not to scratch where her new bras made her itch. When Danielle started receiving phone calls, David was afraid he would use the wrong pronouns so he would use no pronouns at all. "Down by the pool," he would say, "Gone shopping," or 'Not home."

Danielle told me about a 21-year old man, a neighbor in the apartment complex, who took her to the store to get hair spray. "I told him that I have two big brothers who are very protective so I couldn't mess around much," she said. "He is cute, but kind of nerdy. He would make a good friend, but that's all."

I was sure my new daughter was going to get her heart broken, but Danielle was thrilled to meet boys who thought she was a girl. One night when I called, Danielle was out on a "date" with the neighbor. When he came for Danielle, Denise wrote down his address and phone number. The boys were still worried about her, and Ben waited up for her to get home. David decided that before he dated a girl, he would ask to see one of those cute, naked baby pictures. He wasn't sure he wanted to date a transsexual.

David and Ben discussed how to tell their father. They thought of a scheme to soften the blow. They would tell him that David was gay, Ben was a crossdresser, and Daniel was transsexual. Then when he learned the truth, that only Daniel was transsexual, he would be relieved that only one of them had a problem. They laughed and talked about what they thought their father's reaction would be. They never carried out the scheme, but I was thankful my kids could handle this unique situation with humor and common sense.

When Danielle had been in Arizona for only two weeks, David told me the situation was a little stressful, and he was ready for Danielle to return home. Grieving is part of the family's adjustment process when a child comes out as gay or transsexual, and David expressed that sentiment to me when he said, "I feel like my brother has died and I don't know who this new person is." David also felt that it was partly his fault because he had been there when his brother was growing up and he must have done something wrong.

Several times I thought, "I just want my Daniel back." I secretly hoped that Danielle would call and say that she had changed her mind and was going to be my little boy again. I wanted to walk away from all these new problems, and go on with life as it was before. However there were so many things to deal with that I did not have much time for grieving.

My greatest sorrow was in knowing the hardships that lay ahead for my new daughter. I could see it was going to be a long road, and we didn't have a map to follow. I wondered if I would be strong enough to handle this new situation. I asked myself again and again, "Is a mother's love enough?"

* * * * *

While all my children were in Phoenix, I set out to look for information, and my first stop was the Gay and Lesbian Center. Until the moment that Daniel revealed that he was a girl, I was resigned to the fact that he was gay so I expected that I would contact the Center sometime.

14

Is a mother's love enough?

When I was young, my experiences with gays had always been positive. "Uncle Bob" was close to our family and was also the father of one of my best friends. We knew he was gay, but also knew he was a good, dependable person and an important adult in our lives.

A classmate and his twin sister were my best friends during high school. Phil came out to me years later when he explained that he left the church because Christians disapprove of gay people. When I visited him in San Francisco, he lived with two male friends in a beautifully decorated apartment where they all shared the homemaking responsibilities. I noticed the peaceful, caring and quiet atmosphere that pervaded their home, very different from the stressful, bitter and controlling relationships that I had seen in many heterosexual homes. A highly respected teacher in my parochial high school was gay, but we didn't know it at the time. He taught English and made it interesting and challenging. He was married and his children were part of our social circle. Years later I visited him when I learned that he was dying of AIDS, and found that he was still interested in new thoughts and projects. I shared with him my concern for my youngest son.

These three men, as well as all the other gays and lesbians I knew, seemed to be exceptionally fine people. When I believed that Daniel was gay, I hoped he would be a wonderful human being also. I did not blame myself for I had raised all three boys the same way. As early as age five, I recognized Daniel was effeminate and different from other boys, but I knew he did not choose to be that way. It is my belief that some people are born gay just as I was born with curly hair and poor eyesight. I did not feel Daniel was influenced by an outside source, nor did I believe he was sinning.

Fortunately I had read that the hormones to which it is exposed in utero determine the gender of the unborn fetus. All babies start out as female. An infinitesimal amount of male hormone at exactly the right time is necessary for the normal development of male sex organs, and the male pattern of thinking. On rare occasions something goes wrong. There may be enough male hormone to produce male sex organs, but it may not be in sufficient quantity to push the brain into the male pattern of behavior. Although I was surprised and a little shocked to learn that Daniel was transsexual, I think it was easier for me to accept because I knew he was born that way.

* * * * *

I was on the verge of tears on that first visit to the Gay and Lesbian Center, and was thankful to meet a friendly and sympathetic female intern counselor. When I asked for guidance in helping a boy who wanted to be a girl, she could be of little assistance because she admitted she knew almost nothing about the subject. She praised me as a wonderful mother for wanting to help my child, and made a future appointment with a staff psychologist who had experience with transsexuals. She also gave me the phone number of a local support group for transsexuals and crossdressers, called Neutral Corner.

My next stop was the hospital library where I found articles about the use of hormones, and the actual mechanics of sex reassignment surgery. One study hypothesized that transsexuals tend to have more brothers than sisters, and are further down in the birth order. Another theorized that some deficiencies in the womb can result in the birth of a transsexual. One article told of following a group of transsexuals through a spiritual, body and mind transformation with rights of passage. There is little information about transsexuals after surgery because many blend into society and just get on with their lives - they seldom come back to report to the researchers. There were a few outdated psychological studies of children who had gender dysphoria, based on small research samples. But there was no advice for me. I needed a

How to raise a perfect transsexual.

book with step by step instructions - How To Raise a Perfect Transsexual - that might say, "When your teenager tells you he is transsexual, you should do this, this, and this."

The local University hospital informed me that specialists charge $100 an hour, and it would probably take two hours to arrive at a diagnosis. Children's Hospital essentially told me the same, and the local state mental health agency had no specialists. I soon understood that the financial arrangements were of utmost importance, for the first question at all the medical facilities was, "What kind of insurance do you have?" I felt I was all on my own. No one knew what to do, but they would try to figure it out for an outrageous price.

At that time, I was newly connected to the computer world, but even if I had surfed the web there would have been little information available about teens with gender dysphoria. Although my friends and relatives knew no more than I did, it was comforting to talk to them. My mother and my older sister were supportive and reassuring. My mother's reaction when she heard was, "Aha! Of course! That explains so many things."

My Mexican friend and "commadre" Chula (Daniel's godmother), was not surprised about Daniel for she recognized that he walked like a girl when he was only two years old. She had no problem understanding and accepting the situation, and had even read articles in Mexican magazines about transsexuals. She expected trouble with Daniel's father because of his macho attitude. "Since he has never helped with the children," she said, "he better be nice or not say anything at all."

The first breakthrough came with my counseling appointment at the Gay and Lesbian Center. The experienced counselor looked like a hippie with his earring, a beard, a pipe in the pocket of a his Hawaiian shirt, and sandals. He knew of only a few teen transsexuals and even fewer who had gone through sex reassignment surgery, but he answered many of my questions: he doubted that it was just a phase that Daniel was going through; it would not be easy to get hormones from a medical doctor or endocrinologist for a minor; street hormones are dangerous although some have resorted to them to save money; hormones would stop some of the hair growth and electrolysis would also help; most of the effects of taking hormones would disappear when they were discontinued. The success of the transsexual depends somewhat on how well he passes as a female, and the counselor thought he could tell by looking at a picture of Daniel whether he would pass well or not. He asked about Daniel's build and his father's height. I was not worried about him passing because I had already seen Daniel as a girl, and knew that he looked incredibly feminine.

He informed me that several places in the United States perform reputable sex reassignment surgery at a cost of approximately $10,000, and hormone therapy would probably cost $100 a month. That information was important because I would have to find a way to handle the expenses.

The hormonal and surgical treatment of persons with gender dysphoria is strictly regulated by guidelines formulated by a group of psychiatrists, physicians and other caregivers in 1979. These Standards of Care mandated by the Harry Benjamin International Gender Dysphoria Association *(or HBIGDA; today it is called the World Professional Association for Transgender Health or WPATH)* specify that a licensed clinical behavioral scientist (psychologist, counselor, psychiatrist, or clinical social worker) with proven competence in the field must be closely involved before sex reassignment surgery may be permitted. These guidelines are not written in any law, but with only a few surgeons doing sex reassignment, all of who agree to these guidelines, they might as well be law.

The first step requires one of the above professionals to evaluate the person with gender dysphoria over a period of three months before giving a referral for hormone therapy. A year of living full time as the opposite sex is required during which time the person must live and work or go to school in the new gender role before evaluation for surgery is made. Continued contact with the therapist should be maintained during that year because the authorization of two therapists is necessary before the sex reassignment surgery may be considered.

I wasn't ready to think about surgery. I had more urgent needs, such as finding the best way to help my teenager now. This first counselor seemed to be a caring person, and someone with whom I felt comfortable. He said he would be glad to talk to Daniel, but was not set up to write a letter recommending surgery. His services were on donation basis or were free through the Gay and Lesbian Center.

A man from the Neutral Corner support group phoned me in response to my call. The group had no teen information on hand, and he knew of no other transsexual as young as my child. He invited me to attend their support meeting, and to look through their library. As a result of that contact, the wife of a crossdresser called me. She had found out her husband was crossdressing a year or so after their marriage, but with love and counseling they managed to deal with it. Even their two children knew about their father and seemed to be handling it well. A priest told her that crossdressing was not a sin if her husband was not hurting anyone. She was very supportive and encouraging, and although our situations were completely different, it was good to talk to a person with an appreciation for the problems we faced. It was comforting to know that real people had struggled through something similar and continued to live productive lives.

Most of the transsexual information that I found pertained to adults, so I felt I was reinventing the wheel. Parents who had dealt with the same situation could be very helpful. What had they found that worked? What mistakes did they make? What did they do about school? How can parents help?

I knew that I must accept this child as a girl even though I had no idea how to raise a girl, much less a transsexual girl, but

I would do my very best to make a good life for her. A change in my thinking and speaking would be necessary to accommodate a teenage daughter. I vowed that by the time she came back from Arizona, I would be able to use her new name and female pronouns. To practice, I chanted to myself, "I have a new daughter. Her name is Danielle. She is really cute. I love her." The hardest word for me to feel comfortable with was "daughter," since I had always used masculine terms for my children - "Let's go guys. My boys. Hey, little man, none of that." I started using the terms "children and kids" instead of "sons and boys." During that time when I was struggling with gender issues, it gave me peace to think of my child as an angel - pure, innocent and lost, neither male nor female. I even wondered if there might be a reason in the bigger scheme of things, that I was given this child. The thought "Why me?" did occur, but the answer also came right away. "Because you can! "

It was my determination to allow Danielle to set the pace for her future - I would neither push her nor slow her down. It would be my responsibility to provide her with as much information as possible, to discuss options with her, and to pay the bills for any therapy or surgery. I also vowed that our home, wherever it was, would be her sanctuary from the world, a place where she would be safe with no stress or disapproval from me. She would be welcome to go everywhere with me, just as she had in the past: I would not hide her or be ashamed of her.

While Danielle was experimenting with new things in Phoenix, I attended a birthday party where the guest of honor knew of the recent developments concerning Danielle, but the rest of the group did not. When the other guests inquired about my boys I found it difficult to say anything. I made numerous trips to the powder room to dry my eyes.

There were several toddlers in the room, and I heard the mothers exchanging stories about their little boys. I wanted to say, "You **think** they are boys." When I saw a little boy with a pretty face, I wondered about his true identity. My perspective of the whole world had changed. My sister does ultrasound examinations of prenatal infants, and often tells the parents the gender based upon the genitalia that she sees. I thought to myself, "Every parent should be given a disclaimer saying that the fetus has male genitals, but the real gender may not be apparent for years to come."

The support group Neutral Corner has monthly meetings for people with gender issues. The first time I attended I sat in the parking lot for some time trying to build up enough courage to go inside. I was apprehensive about the people I would meet. Finally I went in motivated by the hope of finding answers to some of my questions. I admit that I was also curious to see what transsexuals looked like.

I could not tell which ones were crossdressers or transsexuals, or if those that appeared to be men were really males. It was very difficult to talk to anyone because I discovered that all my conversation starters were based on the person's gender. When meeting men in the past, I first tried to find out if they were single or otherwise eligible, and then talked about their work, sports, cars, or computers. When I met a woman, we talked clothes, kids, work, or men. When the gender was unknown, I struggled to make conversation. I had to rethink what I knew about gender, things that I had previously taken for granted.

After a few minutes, a person appearing to be a male introduced himself to me, said he was a crossdresser, but not dressed tonight, and inquired as to the reason I was there. It was soon evident to him that I could hardly talk without crying, so he changed the subject to politics, and then health-care and other gender-neutral subjects. He was a good conversationalist, intelligent, and a very nice person from all appearances. He did not seem to be odd, or weird, or any of the other things that I had feared I would find at the meeting.

Then a male and female couple revealed to me that she was a male to female transsexual (MtoF) and he was a female to male transsexual (FtoM). Recently they had gone through the gender transition together. They did not know of any young transsexual, nor had they had experience with the schools, but they gave me names of counselors and endocrinologists, and expressed support as I endeavored to help my new daughter. I was happy to discover a nice group of people in attendance who talked about computers, families, and fashion, and I began friendships that night that were of great help to me as I journeyed through a new and unfamiliar territory.

As the evening progressed I was introduced to everyone, and I learned that many of them were successful business people with supportive spouses. Some were crossdressers in female garb, and some were in "drab" which meant they were not dressed as females that night. I learned to tell the difference. Others were MtoFs or FtoMs, but to my surprise and pleasure, most appeared to be happy and well adjusted. Some of the women were very fashionably attired, while I was dressed as usual without earrings, nail polish, or high-heels. They warmly included me in their friendly community, and gave me several books to read from their library. It was interesting to find books on ancient Greek mythological figures that were transsexual and were not treated as if they had a mental illness. The American Indians also had many transsexuals in their tribes who were treated with respect as leaders and teachers because they could see the world from both the feminine and masculine point of view. Traditional Indian society was also very accepting of children deciding which gender, or gender roles they wished to follow. Although the books pertained mostly to adults, I read them anyway. I wanted to learn everything I could on the subject. That experience with Neutral Corner gave me the first glimmer of hope that there might be a happy and successful future for Danielle.

* * * * *

On the way to the airport to pick up my new daughter when she returned from Phoenix, I wondered if I would recognize her. Would she really be a cute teenage girl? I needn't have worried, for she looked adorable to me - a little garish perhaps in the dress and make-up but definitely an attractive female. She was a little tentative about how I would accept her. When I hugged her and let her know that I loved tier, one of the first things she said to me was, "I can't go back to school as a boy. I am too happy as a girl to ever go back." I had already come to the same conclusion. She thanked me over and over for letting her be a girl, and told me how much she loved her brothers and Denise for helping her so much.

After a few weeks it became evident to all who knew Danielle that this change was a wonderful and happy process for her. She was bubbly, exuberant and optimistic about her new life, as the person who had been hidden inside began to emerge. She began letting go of the male role she had tried to maintain. She still had demons of the boy sitting on her shoulder always whispering that the male was still present, but they were becoming quieter. As she became more confident that others were seeing a girl, she let more of her beautiful character blossom and be exposed to the world. It was a celebration of life!

PART II........LEARNING

The next few weeks before school started, Danielle stayed close to home and very close to me. It was as if she had regressed to infancy and was bonding with me. She wanted to sit by me, sleep in my room, and be with me all the time. She needed many hugs and frequent reassurance. How could a child in these circumstances survive if there was no one there to hug her? She returned to her independent teenage self after a month or so.

Some transsexuals in Neutral Corner referred us to Mr. Hunter as the best counselor in the community. I went to the first appointment with Danielle because I didn't want to turn my new daughter over to a stranger who might convince her that she was crazy so that he could then cure her, or one that would come between us. Danielle wore very feminine attire, but was still in her garish phase - tight, short, loud - exaggerated but very cute. The therapist talked to us about our situation a little, but mostly told us about all of his experiences. He inquired whether Danielle was traumatized at an early age for he claimed to have done research to prove his theory that transsexualism is caused by trauma to children under 31 months of age. Daniel was one year old at the time of the flood, and I thought his verbal skills had been affected. He stopped making sounds at all, and only smiled, cried, and pointed until he was three. Whether he was influenced by early trauma made little difference at this point, as I wanted to know what to do now.

Counselor Hunter gave us a Personal History form to fill out and return to him with $150.00. He told us someone else would review it. There would also be psychological testing down the road that would cost $700.00, but we were not to worry about that yet. When the interview was over, he didn't tell us when he wanted to see Danielle again. He did, however, warn us to be careful. Apparently most transsexuals are beaten up at least once by a date if he learns of her past.

We discovered that the questionnaire dealt mostly with adult issues such as marriage, children, sex, and work. There was only a small part about family, growing up, and school that we could fill out, but we returned the form with the money. We never did find out who was reviewing this questionnaire for him. Mr. hunter called me a month later and referred us to an endocrinologist.

We were nearing the end of the summer and had to find some way of getting Danielle into school. It was obvious to me that she would have a better chance if she went to a new school. From past experience I had learned some secrets about getting a child into a specific school in our district. The best way was to move into the neighborhood near the school. There were at least two schools with waiting lists that did not take students from the neighborhood, but if you were the right race you might be bussed from one neighborhood to another, depending on the racial balance the school was trying to achieve. I had played the race game several times with the older boys. Since my children are one-half Hispanic and the other half a mixture of European races, I would choose whichever race was needed for a given situation. On several occasions I tried to do away with race questions altogether, for I objected to choosing either Hispanic or Caucasian. A student could not be registered as mixed racial origin even though he was, nor could he be just American.

27

Finding a school that would be safe for Danielle was uppermost in my mind. When I asked Mr. Hunter about schools, he advised me to call school principals and explain the situation. When I found a friendly person, I could register Danielle in that school.

Following his advice was not easy because the schools were not in session during the summer. Most of the administrators were gone and would not be back until just before school started. Time was running out, and if I had to move, I wanted to get started.

I decided to go directly to the top and call the school district office. There were all kinds of "touchy-feely" committees promoting student wellness, self-esteem, and equity, so I thought they would surely be able to help Danielle. After being transferred from department to department, it seemed the person who normally handled this situation was on vacation. I was finally connected to Ellen.

"What is the school district's policy for dealing with a transsexual student?" I asked.

She asked several questions and then put me on hold while she talked to her boss. When she came back on the phone she said, "Our policy is that we can not discriminate."

"That is not much help."

She said again, "All I can say to you is that we can not discriminate." It sounded as if she wanted to say more.

I hung up in tears of anger and frustration. If they could not discriminate then my "girl" could be in the boy's physical education classes or with the girls, and the school authorities could not do anything about it. Perhaps, if they understood the situation, they would not want her in either PE class. I would wait a few more days for someone to return who supposedly knew more about placing a special student.

After many frustrating calls, I was able to set up an appointment to discuss the matter with a school official face-to-face. I went to the appointment with little hope of receiving

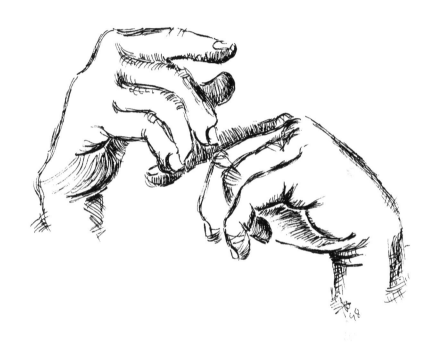

Our Policy is that we cannot discriminate.

help because this official and I had done battle before over the race issue. A few years before he told me that the school district would take me to court and designate one race for my boys since I was refusing to specify one race for them. He didn't follow through on that threat, and I hoped that he did not remember me or the heated words that we exchanged at that time.

To my surprise, he was cordial and appeared genuine in his desire to help me. (Apparently he did not remember our previous encounter.) However, he had no previous experience with a situation like this. Upon inquiry, the computer department informed him that a student's name could not be changed unless the birth certificate was changed. I knew that the name on a birth certificate can be changed, but the gender cannot be changed until after sex reassignment surgery.

He told me about the alternative school programs available in the school district. One was home schooling, but I was not interested in that. There was a program mostly for troubled teens where they could go at their own speed, that wouldn't do either. Danielle was not a troubled teen and I had heard only negative reports about this program. The third possibility was a small alternative school that he said was "pretty laid back" with few rules, but promoted student responsibility. There were some gays and lesbians attending who had not been successful in other schools. The PE program was informal, so the students wore their regular school clothes. This seemed to be the right place to put Danielle, so I filled out the necessary forms. I told him I needed to know soon because I preferred to live close to the school rather than have her bussed across town, and it would be necessary to move. We left on good terms. I didn't even cry.

A few hours later he called with bad news. There was a two-year waiting list for entrance to the alternative school. "Is there any other school that you might consider?" he asked.

I said, "If you can find a place where she will be protected from being beaten, or made fun of, and preferably, where she won't have to take PE, let me know. Since the school principals aren't around yet, it will be hard to talk to them."

He added, "I need to talk to one other person about the alternative school. Maybe there is some hope of getting her in if that person talks to the principal."

So it was still a very frustrating waiting game, with time getting shorter. At the beginning of August, I had given my 30 days notice to the apartment manager, so we had to move soon.

In talking to friends and teachers, I discovered there were quite a few of the teachers' children in this alternative school program. I wondered how long they had been on the "list." A week later, when I was reaching the end of my patience, I talked to David about the alternative school where I thought Danielle would be safe. My plan was to ask the school district to provide me with information on the length of time every student in the school had been on the waiting list. Then I would say I thought they were playing favorites and would loudly demand justice.

David said, "Mother, Mother. Go down to the school district again and tell them you are on the verge of going crazy because you are so worried about your new daughter. You don't want her to be hurt or commit suicide and you don't know what to do and pour on a few tears. "

Although I hate to stoop to such feminine tactics, I did what he said. The tears did come easily, and it worked. School administrators came back from vacation, strings were pulled, and they finally told me I could register Danielle the next Friday. They suggested I register her by her new name and not give too much information. The school principal knew about Danielle's situation, and suggested that the school guidance counselor be told also. He also told me that another transsexual student had attended the school the year before, so I asked if there was any way that I could talk to the parents. The school administrator agreed to give the parents my number, and they could contact me if they wanted to talk to me. It seemed that the school district actually had a heart after all.

While Danielle was having her first appointment with the endocrinologist, I registered her for school. There were the usual numerous and redundant forms to be filled out, and the request for previous records. I told the registration clerk that Danielle had been to school in Canada, and I did not have the address with me. This was partly true for she had attended a few months of school in Canada while living with my brother a year or two earlier. Danielle and I had decided to change her birth date by a year so when her previous name and her new name appeared together on the computer listing, it would not be a cause for suspicion. We had doctored the name on the immunization card by adding the two more letters of her new name to the handwritten form. And this time I didn't make a fuss about the race question.

We forgot to change dates on the immunization papers, and that came back to haunt us a year later when someone noticed she was immunized before she was born. I claimed I just couldn't keep track of all my children's birthdays.

In my own mind, when I tried to justify the lying about names and gender, I decided it was necessary to make the corrections now because the true facts were not known when she was born. I began to call it truthing - the truth as I saw it. Sometimes you have to do what you have to do. Getting her safely situated was more important to me than the information the school officials or the state bureaucrats needed to know. When we claimed Danielle was a new student, all her previous records went to the unclaimed record file, wherever that is.

There were other reasons to be apprehensive about Danielle's schooling, for Daniel could never quite keep up with his class in school. Even during his pre-school years, it was evident that he had trouble with numbers and money. He wanted to play card games and was quick to learn the rules, but could not count the spots on cards above six. When he went to kindergarten he could only identify his lunch money as the big coin, the middle sized, and the little one - meaning a quarter, nickel and dime. We thought he was colorblind because he could not learn the names of colors, although he noticed and remarked about colors and textures more than most children his age. When he was asked what he liked about the new kindergarten he was attending, he said, "I like it because it has such nice colors." On the first day of school, he had noticed that the door to each room around the courtyard was painted a different pastel color.

Even though the school promoted him, I held Daniel back to repeat the first grade. He was still struggling with the letters of the alphabet, but not because he didn't try. He loved his teacher and she loved him, and there was no disruptive behavior. He seemed bright enough, but because of his confusion about letters and numbers, we suspected some learning disability. I had him tested by an educational psychologist at a university. The results were that he had no learning disability, but was not as mature as one would expect at his age. He was tested again at the end of the second year of first grade when he had still not mastered the basics. The result was the same - he would be all right when he matured a little more.

As he progressed in school he continued to have difficulty with letters and numbers, and particularly in learning the multiplication tables. He would learn the sixes, but by the time he learned the sevens, he had forgotten the sixes no matter how much I helped him or how hard he tried. He was such a loving and happy boy that I couldn't get impatient with him. He did very well with coloring and crafts, and had an extraordinary appreciation for art and beauty. He was very sensitive to the feelings of others, and always noticed when someone felt sad, ill, or unhappy. I had read that such sensitivity is common in girls, who are able to pick up subtle clues and notice a small change of facial expressions, but is unusual in a boy. But Daniel had no idea about yesterday or tomorrow, or the meaning of night and morning. He used the words interchangeably. He liked to cook and learned to read enough to follow a recipe, but I didn't think he would ever learn more fractions than those used in the cookbook.

Daniel's feminine demeanor and behavior had, however, been of some concern to a few of the teachers and counselors in the school system.

"Your son swishes when he walks," said Daniel's third grade teacher. I knew she meant that his hips swayed and he walked like a girl. "Every time the children are walking in line to and from the classroom, I tell him to quit swishing."

I knew he "swished" when he walked. I was just sorry that Daniel had to be hassled by this thoughtless teacher. I told her, "If it is not getting in the way of his learning, please ignore it. Please stop pointing it out and just leave him alone."

She seemed to have little understanding of children, and we had no choice of teachers because she was the only one for that grade. So we moved to another school.

It was a school counselor who called the next year. "Do you know your son is playing with girls on the playground at recess?" I thought, "Why is that harmful? Girls are people, too, and why should it matter that he wants to play with them.?"

The counselor went on to say. "Your son has been overheard saying that he wants to be a girl."

"What do you think I should do about that?" I asked.

"Well, don't encourage it," was his answer. "Ten is way too young to know about sexual orientation." I did mention the conversation to Daniel, but he evaded the subject.

When Daniel was in eighth grade, I was called to the school for a conference with both the school nurse and the counselor.

"Your son needs counseling," was their advice to me.

"Why do you think so?"

"Because he cries when the other children make fun of him."

It sounded to me as if they were trying to treat the symptoms without treating the disease. I figured they were advising counseling for Daniel so as to change his behavior because they could not control the children who were teasing and calling him names. They never came right out and said he was gay, but they beat around that bush for a while.

When I asked for a referral to a good counselor, they did not know of any, and the school district had no such counselors.

* * * * *

When I talked to the endocrinologist after Danielle's first visit, I was pleased to find that he had a positive attitude although he had not seen many transsexuals as young as Danielle. He gave her the prescription for hormones, and had blood drawn for lab work. Danielle was thrilled to have reached that important milestone. In the waiting room were two persons I had previously met at a support meeting, and they were very much impressed that Danielle passed so well already. Comments like these made me teary-eyed, but I tried to keep from crying in front of Danielle so as not to worry or stress her.

From the doctor's office, we went to the new apartment to sign papers, then we headed for the drug store. I had just said to Danielle, "I can't handle anything more today," when I noticed that the gas gauge was on empty.

It had been a good day overall, but dealing with school registration, appointments, forms, money, and decisions had drained me emotionally. At the service station, I went to use the phone to answer a page while Danielle pumped the gas. When I got out of the car I locked the keys inside. That was the last straw. I walked toward the back of the station, sat down in a flowerbed, and cried and cried. Poor Danielle! The men at the station were trying unsuccessfully to unlock the car while casting quick glances my way wondering if they had a crazy person on their hands. Meanwhile, Danielle was cool and calm. She called the Automobile Association and soon the mechanic arrived to unlock the door. By then I had gotten the storm out of my system and we went on to get her hormones - ironically, the same hormones I was struggling to keep under control. Although we had been told that hormones would not make any immediate changes, she was still very anxious to get started. We have since had several good laughs about my sitting in the flowerbed at the gas station crying. The way she handled the stressful situation and a mother "on the edge" demonstrated her maturity.

We had to solve the problem of filling Danielle's empty bra. Teen girls pad with Kleenex, and there are prosthetics to use following a mastectomy, but Danielle needed something in between. Even the bras with the most padding were not full enough to suit her. We tried several homemade remedies such as shoulder pads cut down to the right size, but Danielle had the feeling that people could tell because they didn't look real. She thought people were looking at her breasts everywhere she went.

What were others using full time and successfully? At my first meeting with the Neutral Corner support group, I asked two friendly people how they padded their bras. They realized it was a very serious question, and gave me good information. The pads are called breast forms. There are several options on the market, and they each used a different kind. Since breast forms are expensive and not easy to find, they volunteered to meet with Danielle and show her the kind of undergarments they wore. These two people accepted my invitation for coffee later in the week. One person came dressed as a very proper mature female, and the other in business attire with white shirt, tie, and his boobs in a box. The scene was so humorous to me that I could hardly keep from giggling. Two grown men, one dressed as a woman and one as a businessman showing what looked like a teenage girl the differences in fake breasts. But I knew this was a crucial matter.

One set of breast forms was silicone and looked much like a post-mastectomy breast prosthesis. It felt best to the touch. The other was a breast shaped pocket with little round bags filled with sand. The breast shape could be enlarged by adding more sandbags or made smaller by removing some of the little bags. We chose the second type, called "Bosom Buddies" because it appeared to be more durable which would probably be best for an active teenager. We learned how to purchase them at a cost of just over $100.00 a set.

When Danielle started wearing "Bosom Buddies" she still felt insecure as they seemed to move around. She was afraid they might come loose from her bra and become lodged where she did not want them. To solve that problem, I sewed snaps on the cloth outer pocket and placed snaps in her bra to match. These have worked satisfactorily for more than two years now. As the hormones kicked in and she grew small tender breasts of her own, she just took out some of the little sand bags. These were difficult to use for swimming because she only had one set and they required several hours to dry.

I will long remember and be grateful for the help that those two crossdressers gave us. It was comical, but most beneficial.

Danielle used tight girdle type underwear, sometimes two or three pair on top of each other to give her confidence that hidden parts would stay hidden. The term for this is called tucking. Hormones do help in keeping things under control as well.

Just before school started, the parents of a transsexual teen the same age as Danielle called to invite us to their home, but I went alone to protect Danielle from any unforeseen difficulty.

Laura and her parents showed a great interest in Danielle, and Laura was very disappointed that Danielle had not accompanied me. Her mom and step-dad seemed pleased to talk with me as we discussed the way we had each raised our special child. We agreed that there was no reason for us to feel guilty. Laura's mom had wanted a girl, but knew that simply wishing did not cause her son to be a girl. I, on the other hand, had always been glad that I had boys.

As we talked, I learned that Laura's favorite movie was Cinderella, while Danielle's was Pretty Woman, both movies showing a woman taking on a new identity. Laura had tried to make her transition while attending her local high school, but when that proved to be unsuccessful she transferred to the same alternative program that Danielle would soon be starting. Since Laura did not do very well at that school either, she was doing home schooling. She was very frank in explaining the changes that hormones had made in her body - enlarged breasts, redistribution of fat, and no erections. Luckily she had never had much facial hair.

It was reassuring to me to see her parents handling the situation with understanding. They made it all seem so easy. They were not involved in the transgender community.

When I returned home and gave Laura's telephone number to Danielle, she immediately phoned her. They talked for hours that first day and they have been talking ever since. They shared clothes, makeup tips, and friends. Laura had a collection of Barbie dolls that kept them occupied. Laura had blond hair, a low sexy voice and looked like a movie star. And she liked to change the color and style of her hair weekly. She seemed to need more attention and excitement than Danielle, so she always knew where things were happening, and wanted to be there. She was more emotional than Danielle, and was quicker to tell people that she was transsexual, but didn't "out" Danielle - that is, didn't reveal that Danielle was also a transsexual. I sometimes wondered if Laura's influence was entirely good for Danielle, but thought perhaps Danielle was good for Laura. They formed a close bond because they shared a unique experience.

38

As soon as Danielle got her driver's license, she and Laura did something together every weekend. They explored the coffee shops in the gay-friendly part of town, but Danielle quickly tired of that because the men paid no attention to her. They also visited the nightclubs in Mexico where Danielle could flirt her way in with no identification.

I didn't see Laura's parents often, but we knew a lot about each other's teenager, and we knew where to call when they were late getting home. When Danielle was out too late, I just hoped she was having fun because she deserved some happiness. The girls spent many nights at the home of one or the other - that was their story anyway. I hoped that they wouldn't get in trouble with the law, because in our town there is a law against crossdressing during the committing of any other crime with the intent of fraud. Most jails will put pre-operative transsexuals with those of like genitalia, in other words both Danielle and Laura would have been put in with men.

Danielle never felt a need for the support groups with which I was involved, but she and Laura stopped by occasionally to humor me and show off how well they were doing. They enjoyed being told how cute they were.

I felt that Laura's parents had a tendency to spoil her, and realized that I did the same with Danielle. One instance was while we were shopping for jewelry for Danielle's prom. She liked a set that cost $80, and I had justified in my mind that she deserved the expensive jewelry. She then found a very similar set that cost only $20, which we bought. As we left, she said, "Now we can spend the $60 we saved." We didn't, but I thought to myself, she is a true female.

Life had dealt both Danielle and Laura a difficult hand, so as their parents, we wanted to do all we could to make it easier for them.

* * * * *

We had found an apartment that looked like a decent place
to live near the new school, and started the moving process.
We were good at moving because we did it so often.
But this move was different. I had to chuckle to myself
when I realized my attitude toward my daughter had changed.
In the past two moves since Ben and David had left, I had let
my youngest teenage son carry heavy things, and take on the
weighty tasks. Now I kept wanting to tell my new teenage
daughter to be careful when lifting heavy items, and I was
willing to shoulder more of the load to spare her. Until then, I
had been unaware of such gender-biased attitudes, but now
they popped up once in a while. Danielle, on the other hand,
felt just as strong as ever, and was just as willing to do her
share and more to spare me the heaviest work. She wanted us
to make the move by ourselves without any help from men.
She had not adopted the attitude of a helpless, defenseless
female, but rather wanted to be an independent woman. I had
prided myself on having this same attitude, but that day I
would have gladly accepted help in moving.

Another instance of having to examine my attitude toward
my new daughter was that I did not want her to drive in
Mexico even though her brothers had at the same age.

As the first day of school neared, I was very apprehensive
for Danielle. One of the reasons we chose this new school was
because of its open campus policy, so she could come home
anytime she felt uncomfortable. She was still self-conscious,
and she felt she had to come home at noon and shave. She
wasn't self-conscious about her wardrobe however. She had all
of the latest fashions and wearing these clothes helped boost
her confidence. She was also very unsure of her voice. Since
she has started hormones before a deep male voice evolved,
she had a better chance of maintaining a more feminine voice.

Her voice was at the lower range of female and to my ear, very acceptable, but a source of concern for Danielle.

At the end of that first day of school, I was very much relieved to learn that all had gone well for her. She was happy with the situation, and no one had guessed that she had attended school as a boy the year before. She had the option of using the nurse's restroom, but was afraid it would arouse attention, so she used the girl's restroom. If there was ever a problem, she took comfort in knowing that she could reach me through my pager at any time. Since I am self-employed, I make my own hours and can leave at a moment's notice. She tried not to worry me, but there were several occasions when I went home to be with her. She still needed frequent reassurance and hugs. The hormones seemed to cause a roller coaster of emotions. Some days she just cried. I told her, "Sometimes women have crying days. It is called water build-up, and sometimes you just have to cry before you feel better."

She called me once when she came home early from a school dance because she had a zit on her nose. The next time she danced until they turned out the lights in a new dress she made for the occasion. I was glad that she was having the opportunity to be a girl - zits and all. She and I often went Country Western Dancing together and then, as she met other teens, she attended dances for teens only. When I picked her up one night after a dance, the adult chaperones told me they thought Danielle was a sweetheart and very mature. People often said that about her, and I always thought, " You have no idea." On the way home she told me of an ugly scene that occurred. "Some older girls were mimicking other kids and making fun of them," she said. "They kept pointing at me while I was dancing. I stopped and faced them and told them I was tired of them making fun of everyone. They called me names and asked me to go outside and fight. I told them I didn't want to fight.

Sometimes women have crying days.

I was just tired of them making fun of me because they were jealous of how well I danced." Danielle felt she handled herself well, and thought the other girls made themselves look stupid. They left after making threats to harm her and even kill her. She explained to me, " Fifteen years of pent up anger at people making fun of me came to the surface and I took it all out on those two girls." I was proud of her and sad that her earlier life had been so hard.

* * * * *

My work took me out of town overnight twice a month. I used to leave Daniel alone, but now it was different leaving Danielle. She assured me that she would be all right alone at night, but I wanted to be near to protect her. When I couldn't be there, I arranged for friends to come stay with her.

She had a great desire to have a girl's bed. I didn't know that beds had gender, but we went looking for a feminine bed. We found a single waterbed with a pretty headboard with mirrors and shelves. I had to admit that it did look as if it belonged in a girl's room. When we got it home, we struggled unsuccessfully to put it together, so we finally swallowed our pride and asked for help from a man. My sister's son, who is the same age as Danielle, sent her a pretty blown-glass bottle from a trip to Europe, which she put on this headboard. His gesture of love and acceptance meant a great deal to Danielle.

The first school year went quite smoothly, and she made amazing advances in her school studies. I was sure that I would have to help her with algebra, but she did it by herself from the beginning. Her English and writing improved, and she advanced by leaps and bounds in all her work. It was as if someone had turned on the lights. Things were suddenly making sense. The teachers were talking her language. Now she could think about school and learning instead of being overloaded by unexplained feelings and emotions.

One day I met some of Danielle's teachers in a coffee shop before school. They were very complimentary: they praised me for the way my daughter had been raised. When they told me what a good teenager she was, I had to bite my tongue. They never could have imagined the handicap with which Danielle was coping. It became a part of my life to accept the praise without revealing her secret.

I wanted everyone to share with me the joy and beauty of this new person, but Danielle didn't want everyone to know so I had to keep it to myself around her friends, her teachers and the neighborhood. The Neutral Corner support group was one place where I could share my feelings and pride in Danielle's accomplishments. They knew what a struggle it had been, and I knew they could keep secrets. I hoped my need to tell others would eventually fade - but it hasn't.

* * * * *

Physical Education had been a major concern when we were choosing a high school for Danielle. Counselor Hunter recommended that we have a family doctor write a medical reason such as a heart problem to get her excused. We have a doctor in our family who said he would be glad to do that for Danielle, but as it turned out we did not need to go that route. At the alternative school, students were not required to dress down for PE except to wear tennis shoes. As Danielle gained confidence in herself, she even began to enjoy PE, a class that she had never liked before.

She once mentioned the Presidential Fitness testing program, "I am trying to do more than is required by the girls because I feel like I am cheating a little." She was still adjusting her thinking to accommodate this new gender - relating her performance to the previous male requirements, even though she looked like a female.

The second year she wanted to attend a mainstream school and be in regular PE classes, changing into PE clothes with other girls in the locker room. I wanted to save her from possible embarrassment or problems, but again I bit my tongue and let her attempt anything that she was brave enough to try. I did not want to slow her down, or make her paranoid because of my fears. Thinking about another mother finding out about Danielle gave me nightmares. If the school district's policy had allowed her to substitute dance for PE, or not to take it at all, I would have been more comfortable. We decided that we could move to another part of town if she were discovered.

We asked about showers before making our final decision about tile Mainstream school. Showering for PE was optional, due to the parents of Eastern religions not allowing their sons and daughters to undress in front of anyone. This was one of the few religious rules that I ever thought made good sense. As far as I am concerned, it is a barbaric practice to have self-conscious teens, at different stages of puberty, undress in front of one another. Danielle wore a halter top over her bra, and her usual girdle type underwear to maintain modesty while she changed.

As the year progressed, she even joined the track and field team in an effort to maintain a healthy body. Again I worried about her competing against other schools because I feared someone might recognize her and object to her running on the girl's team. She did her best, but due to the heavy doses of hormones, she would run out of steam before the end of a race. When I attended track meets, I listened as other mothers talked about the problems they had with their children, but I had to keep quiet about Danielle. I wanted to tell them how proud I was of my unique, amazing teenager, but I remained silent. Talking to a coach about Danielle seemed like a wise thing to do so he would not be blind-sided if any questions arose, but I didn't - and there were no problems.

Danielle noticed that some of the other girls on the track and field team had no more breasts than she did, but she wasn't convinced that she could go without her breast forms.

During two years of trial and error, we found several workable options for a transsexual student facing PE in high school. The district nurse told me that it was easy to be excused from PE in our school district. A student with a health problem, birth defect or other condition causing difficulty in social adjustment could obtain a mental health excuse. No one had volunteered this information to me when we started inquiring about PE. Our district also gives PE credits to students who are doing another physical activity outside of school hours such as swimming or soccer.

Danielle was in a choir class during the second year of high school where the students learned both music and dance in preparation for a show they would put on at the end of the semester. The costume and shoes cost $60.00, and I reluctantly gave her the money.

When the costume arrived, Danielle was upset because the outfit for the girls was so skimpy. The neck was low cut to be worn off the shoulder, and the high cut legs were inadequately covered by a very short skirt. She could not wear her bra or girdle underwear with the outfit, and would feel altogether very uncomfortable. A few inches of material made a big difference in this setting.

I wondered about the judgment of the flaky male teacher who chose the inappropriate costume that definitely did not comply with school regulations. My first impulse was to make war with the school, but Danielle wanted to handle it herself by quitting the class without making waves. She did it her way, but later I did got my two cents in when other questions and concerns about this class arose.

Danielle had to meet some difficult situations, but she seemed to be adjusting well in school. Although she was so brave in some instances, this time she just wanted to walk away.

She showed a surprising maturity by knowing which fights to fight. She chose her wars wisely, differently from the way I chose to fight every battle that came along.

Daniel at 8 years

Daniel at 14 years

Danielle at 15 years

Danielle at 19 years

PART III.......ACCEPTING

During the years since my divorce, I had kept the boys in contact with their Mexican family, and had tried to maintain a civil relationship with their father for the sake of the children. The boys and I went down to visit the Mexican relatives on many special family occasions, and we were always accepted as part of the family. Daniel and his Mexican grandmother had a special bond, so his grandmother was heartbroken when we left to live in the States. Daniel spent several summer vacations with her in Mexico.

Salvador later remarried, moved to California, and had two more children. My boys really liked their half-siblings, and Daniel especially was thrilled to have a half-sister. My children visited their father frequently and even baby-sat the little ones. The stepmother didn't mind having my children around, and my boys would occasionally ride to Mexico with their father and his family to visit relatives.

Danielle's father was a Roman Catholic with little education, and had a closed mind about people whom he considered different. During the transition from Daniel to Danielle, she talked to her father about her feelings, explaining that she was really a girl. She purposely did not dress as a girl during this discussion with him. When she told me about the meeting with her father, she said he had been understanding, and I hoped for the best. Shortly after that, Danielle returned on a bus late one evening from a visit with her Mexican family. I asked Salvador to pick her up at the border because he lived closer than I did. It was the first time he had seen her dressed as a girl. I met them at his house, and watched as Danielle thanked him and tried to hug him as she said good-by. Her father turned away rejecting her. It was apparent from his angry looks at me that he thought I had purposely set up this situation. His apparent understanding about her change disappeared when he actually saw her as a girl.

After that, when Danielle happened to be visiting in the small Mexican town at the same time as her father, he would leave. He once walked out of the Catholic Church when she entered. He did the same when she arrived during a meal at the home of relatives.

On numerous occasions I talked to him about Danielle, and how much it would mean to her if he would see her. I requested he speak to a Catholic priest whom I knew to be understanding of the transsexual community. Her father's response to that was, "Danielle is the one with the problem. She needs to talk to the priest."

Her older brothers also talked to their father and his wife to no avail. After a year or more David and Ben began to distance themselves from their father because of his continued rejection of their sister. Danielle continued to call her father who would talk to her on the phone, but would not visit or meet her, and he didn't attend any of the important events in her life. Even though her heart was breaking, she continued calling him still hoping that she could win him over. She sadly missed her little half-brother and sister. When a new girl baby was born, Danielle was not allowed to get acquainted with her at all.

Her Mexican Grandma tried to ignore the issue until Danielle went to visit her in a frilly dress, with high-heeled boots and a purse.

Her grandmother's first words were, "How come you are carrying a purse?"

It was the first time he had seen her dressed as a girl.

During that visit Danielle and her Grandma laughed and cried together, and Grandma was convinced that Danielle was happier living as a girl. In the same courageous manner, Danielle faced the rest of the family, and the aunts and cousins soon treated her as if she had always been a girl.

One male cousin became very protective and watched out for her safety when he took her to dances and rodeos. She went to the dances in the little town where everyone had known her before as a boy. At first the guys would not ask her to dance, but her cousins did, and soon several others became her friends and danced with her too. Because she was brave and proud, others did not see her as an outcast, and soon she was being treated as a celebrity. She returned from her visits happy but exhausted because it was still stressful for her to be watched all the time.

Her father and one of his brothers continued to reject her, and would not attend family functions if she was going to be there. Her father sent her messages telling her not to attend dances in his hometown, and not to talk to his children if she saw them. She ignored the messages. She was deeply hurt by the strife in the family, and felt that she was the cause.

Again and again I told her, "It is not your fault, and your father is the only one that can stop the strife by changing his attitude."

Her father blamed the rest of the family for accepting her because he felt that she would not have continued her process of becoming female if the whole family had rejected her in the beginning.

Often I am thankful that I did not have to face Daniel's gender problems while living with Salvador because the difficulties of the transition would have been magnified many times over. Trying to protect Danielle and preserve the marriage would have torn me apart.

Because she was brave and proud,
others did not see her as an outcast.

Sometimes I feel sorry for her dad because he is missing out on so much. At other times I hate him for hurting her and being so selfish, thinking only about himself. I cannot understand a parent rejecting a child, especially such a beautiful, kind, and happy child as Danielle. How can he possibly have peace in his heart?

* * * * *

My social outlet for many years has been Community Theater. I do stage managing, and participate in other behind-the-scene activities to make sure the show goes on, but I have no desire to be in the spotlight on the stage.

Among the theater community, I have made several very good friends through the years, and some are gay or lesbian. It was while I was in the middle of rehearsals for "Ten Little Indians," working with my favorite director and several friends that I found out about Danielle. I tried not to let my personal problems interfere with the play, but sometimes I would cry for no apparent reason at all. I finally told my friends in the cast about Danielle because she would be attending rehearsals with me. They had known my boys as they were growing up, and were very interested and supportive when they learned of the situation.

When Danielle went to the theater with me one night, my friends acted as if they had known her as a girl all along - it was no big deal. They even got her name right! One of her favorite actors hugged her and told her she was cute. The actors that did not know her before had no inkling that something momentous was happening.

There were some interesting situations when new actors flirted with Danielle and tried to get better acquainted. Although I wanted to protect her from getting hurt and avoid embarrassment for the actors, there was not much I could do. However, the director once warned a newcomer that Danielle was "jail bait" since she looked so much older than fifteen. I was surprised that my friends who knew about her did not tell any of the other theater people.

Danielle went to an annual awards banquet with me where many of our friends greeted her warmly and gave her compliments on her appearance. One man asked her if hormones had given her that great shape. I thought she would be offended by such a direct question, but she answered in the affirmative and then hugged him.

Later she told me, "He was the only person that actually said anything directly to me about my new situation. That really made me feel good. Everyone else just told me how good I looked, but ignored the real subject."

It was my belief that my **FRIENDS** would understand, and they did.

* * * * *

Daniel had started shaving at age thirteen because he had quite a growth of facial hair - unlike his father and older brothers who had sparse beards. In the past I had remarked that some girls like guys with lots of hair, never realizing what a heartache all that hair caused for Daniel. Just when we were trying to deal with hormones, counseling, moving to a new apartment and a new school, we also had to deal with the matter of removing Danielle's facial hair by electrolysis.

One of our crossdresser friends recommended an electrologist, and Danielle arranged for an appointment. She and I went together for the first meeting where the electrologist explained the procedure, but could not answer all the questions I asked. How long would she have to have electrolysis, and how much would it cost? She said it depends on many variables, including pain threshold, type of skin, and genetic makeup

She further explained that Danielle would eventually need electrolysis around her genitals in preparation for surgery, so she wanted a picture of Danielle without clothes. Danielle didn't seem to mind so I didn't make a big deal out of it, but since then I have learned that taking nude pictures is not an accepted practice. Although the electrologist and I became friends, we never did see or talk about the picture she took that day.

Thus began the many hours Danielle spent in electrolysis, and the many dollars I spent paying for it. Electrolysis is a slow process and some days I was not sure we were making any progress at all. We heard that it might take as many as 300 hours. There were days when Danielle stayed home from school because her facial hair was too long to hide and she couldn't shave the day of an electrolysis appointment. We called them bad hair days. Days when I was out of town, Danielle took the responsibility of getting to her appointment on her own by bus or roller blades.

As I carefully observed the procedure, I thought it might be something that I could do. It would be a great savings to me, and it might eventually become another part time business. Through research, I learned that 600 hours of class and an examination were required for State Board Certification, but the nearest school was 100 miles away. I started the classes just after Danielle had completed her first year of treatment. I enjoyed the training and the hours of practice on Danielle. She taught me to be gentle, patient and careful during the procedure, and to talk to her at the same time. We had many good conversations while I was working on her, and we became even closer as we spent this time together.

Electrolysis is an art form, not a science. The pain, money and time spent in electrolysis weeds out those with just a passing fancy for changing to the opposite gender.

Danielle accompanied me to class on several occasions where the other students were amazed at her feminine appearance. We spent many nights at motels near the classroom to maximize my time at school. I worked at my other contract jobs during the days between classes. I never wasted a minute - a habit that I cultivated while raising my three children.

By the time I finished my classes and the required practice hours, and passed the State Board examination, I had rented an office. My part time electrolysis business grew by word of mouth through the transgender community. They seemed to feel comfortable with me since I knew the problems they were experiencing while in transition. In time my business developed into a haven where the transgender were comfortable and knew they were welcome. My clients started popping in between appointments to network with others in the community. Regularly scheduled social gatherings evolved from this. My efforts seemed to encourage a community spirit among the transsexuals as they became better acquainted and reached out to one another.

The rewards of my business were more than financial. My sister sometimes says to me, "You seem to have made lemonade out of lemons." To which Ben always adds, "Damn good lemonade."

We never did any genital electrolysis on Danielle because we learned from those in our area that had gone through surgery without it, that none of them had complications. There have been a few reports of hair in the new vagina, which is unpleasant, but has not caused other medical problems like infection. There seems to be no consensus among surgeons as to which area requires electrolysis. At this point in time, I think that the cure is worse than the problem.

* * * * *

One of Danielle's friends invited her to go with the Scouts to the Colorado River on a canoe trip. She was to take food, water, and everything she needed for the four days in a small canoe. She was required to learn canoeing and to be able to swim. When I took her to a small lake for the canoeing classes, she was eager to learn and did very well.

The group was to include both Boy Scouts and Girl Scouts, so Danielle would be sleeping in a tent with other girls. The group also included several adults whom I found to be very friendly. I thought it would be wise to tell at least one of them about Danielle, but she did not want me to tell anyone. After discussing the situation at length, we decided that if there was a problem, I could be there in three hours to bring her home.

She was trained in survival techniques and had to pass some swim tests, in case the canoe overturned. Each of the Scouts had to jump into the water fully clothed over a swimsuit, remove their clothes, and swim a lap. They were told not to wear jeans or sweats because they would be too heavy when wet. For the test Danielle chose a pair of nylon jogging pants with elastic around the ankles. I was watching from the bleachers with interest but not concerned because I knew that Danielle was a strong swimmer. She jumped in and almost immediately began to struggle and looked frightened. When she entered the water, her nylon pants immediately filled with water. The nylon material and the elastic around the ankles kept all of the water in her pants causing her to be dragged under. Before I could get out of the bleachers, she turned to the lifeguard and called for help. He went right in and brought her to the edge. It was amazing to me how quickly even a good swimmer could get in trouble in the water.

Since she had satisfactorily completed all the other water activities, the leaders did not make her repeat that test. They did tell her not to wear those pants on the trip. After she stopped shaking and calmed down, we headed for home.

She asked me, "Did you see how cute the lifeguard was? I wonder if he could tell that I was wearing breast forms when he put his arm across my chest."

We bought all the required supplies including a very conservative swimsuit - a one piece, with boy legs, and a high neckline so she could wear her bra. She wore very tight cutoff shorts most of the time, and a shirt tied in front. No matter what she wore, she looked sexy even when nothing was showing but her tummy. We made a little bag for her wet breast forms so she could hang them up to dry over night. She left on the trip, and I tried to keep busy so that I would not worry.

She slept in a tent with four other girls and a female counselor. They went in pairs to visit the bathroom facilities - the bushes - and she was careful to be well hidden. At one of the overnight stops, there were showers. She kept her underwear on while she showered since the curtains were not very substantial.

She had fun on the outing and had no problems, but found canoeing on the river rather boring. It was good for her to participate in the Girl Scout experience as one of the things that girls do. I was sorely tempted to tell the Girl Scouts that they had taken a transsexual with them on the river trip and no harm had been done, but I didn't. At a later speaking engagement, I told the audience about the river trip. A Scout leader came up after the program to tell me that he would have been required to put Danielle in a tent by herself if he had known, even though he was understanding and a crossdresser himself.

* * * * *

Danielle learned about the New Images Theater Group sponsored by Planned Parenthood. They were all teens that did skits and stage plays dealing with teen issues. She auditioned to be part of the troupe. If she was accepted, there would be a stipend of $200.00 a month. Although I worried about the auditions because I feared that she might be very disappointed if she did not get a part, she was very confident that she could do it and would be part of the group.

The would-be actors were asked to portray an animal at the auditions, and Danielle chose to be a cat. Everyone laughed when her imitation sounded like a cat having an orgasm. She was a little embarrassed. There were other impromptu acts required that included singing and dancing. I was very proud of her that she was chosen to be a member of the troupe.

The members of the theater represented ethnic and sexual diversity. They wrote and produced their own skits and they were very well done. Danielle learned about child and sexual abuse, contraception, body parts, counseling, and acceptance of diversity. During a training session on transsexuals, the leader told what she knew, then Danielle added to the information claiming that she had a friend who was transsexual. The group went on camping trips and overnight outings together and became very close. I wanted to tell the leader about Danielle because I thought that this group of kids would be supportive and understanding, but Danielle did not want them to know yet. She seemed more comfortable around people that did not know about her past.

After many performances, when the group had been together almost a year, they went on an overnight trip. The kids became pretty emotional after the performance, and as often happens at a slumber party, they told their secrets to each other. The leader was trying to divide the group into acceptable sleeping arrangements in the one large empty room that was their abode for the night. Each teen had a sleeping bag and none of them were in romantic relationships, but she sent the boys to one corner of the room and the girls to another. One of the girls told the leader that if she was trying to prevent sex, this would not work because at least one of the girls was a lesbian, and at least one of the boys was gay. The leader then attempted to divide the straight and gays from each other. It was at this time that Danielle decided to reveal herself. The leader later told me that she gave up then, and let the kids all sleep together in the middle of the room. She just didn't have the heart to make Danielle sleep in an area all by herself after such an emotional revelation. I was very grateful for such an understanding leader. The others were amazed when they heard. They hugged her and cried with her. Danielle was happy that she had let her friends know about her past, and that they were very supportive..

When Danielle's year with New Images was over, she helped with the training session about transsexuals for the next group. The year with this group was very good for her self-confidence, and I was thankful that she had received a sound education on many controversial issues.

* * * * *

One time Danielle rode to a party with several of her friends, but the boy that drove the car became so drunk that Danielle had to find another way home. Another time she was frightened because the driver was speeding. I was anxious for Danielle to get a driver's license and bought her a used pick-up as soon as she was old enough so as to avoid such uncomfortable and dangerous circumstances. If she were in control of the vehicle she could leave if she found herself in an unsafe or awkward situation. She had more common sense and was more responsible and mature than other teens with whom I had become acquainted.

A new law had just passed in our state requiring every new applicant for a driver's license to show a birth certificate. This was to verify age and citizenship, not gender. I was trying to avoid the government being involved in my child's gender reassignment, so we considered many ways to approach the problem. The State has a protocol for the change of name and sex on a current driver's license. An endocrinologist has to declare on a Department of Motor Vehicle form that the person is living full time as a female and intends to have sex reassignment surgery. I had been told that such medical information is confidential, but any alias will show up on a computer search. It doesn't take a rocket scientist to figure out that if a person has changed from Joe to Jane, that individual is probably a transsexual. I could just see Big Brother with a drawer labeled "Confidential Name Changes (Transsexuals)."

We had several options. One was buying a fake birth certificate. Another was to find an old typewriter with the same print as the original birth certificate and change the information. We tried to generate a computer certificate similar to the current Government Issue. None of these ideas worked, but Danielle found a solution that did work. One day she sat down with my magnifying glasses, and with a pencil put the two extra letters after her male name to feminize it. She wrote "Fe" in front of "Male," darkened the letters slightly to match, and we had just committed a felony. Some would not agree with our methods, but the birth certificate now showed the truth. We just did not have all the information when she was born.

On the way to Department of Motor Vehicles, she said, "I feel like "Thelma & Louise."

I told her, "Don't make a big deal about the birth certificate. Flash one of your wonderful smiles."

She had no problem. They glanced at the date of birth and did not keep a copy. They have no proof showing that she altered the birth certificate, and she has her license showing she is a female, with the name she wants.

When she applied for an Arizona drivers license, they required a Social Security number as identification, but we had not changed the Social Security card. We could have done that quite easily with available forms, but again, we wanted to avoid notifying the government.

Danielle showed her card to the clerk who asked, "Is this an alternative spelling of your name?"

She answered, "Yes," and left it at that.

On another occasion, she had to show her Social Security card for employment in a fast food restaurant. I told her, "Don't make a big deal of it. Just show it like there is nothing special."

When Danielle got home, I asked, "So, how did you do with your Social Security card?"

"They didn't even speak English," she said.

People from other countries do not always know which names are traditionally female or male names, so they didn't recognize any problem.

ON BEING NORMAL

Normal is a word that I try not to use anymore. Danielle met a boy who was attending Narcotics Anonymous for his drug habit. She attended one meeting with him to see what it was all about, and on the way home, he tried to play on her emotions.

"You have a normal life. You have no idea how hard it is to quit drugs."

He didn't get any sympathy from her, as she answered, "I didn't do anything stupid like start drugs in the first place."

And so this boy joined the others that she met along the way that she did not need to know any better.

Although I knew how hard her life was, she just looked like any other teenager. I considered that a real accomplishment.

Normal is just a setting on the washing machine.

FAMILY MEALS

Danielle was on the phone defending our non-traditional meals. I heard her explain to a friend, "MY mother is busy working, and we come and go at different times. We just ate what and when we want and share with each other if we are both home and hungry at the same time."

When the children were young and money was scarce, we ate a lot of tortillas and beans together. As we became more affluent we had more choices, but I had learned that what and when the children wanted to eat did not always fit my schedule or idea of a meal. They did not like casseroles, so when I made one, I had to eat it for days. Hot-dogs or bologna sandwiches every other day didn't do it for me. Sometimes when we were all home at the same time we had a sit-down meal of spaghetti or tacos, foods that we all liked. Danielle had gone through her vegetarian phase, and her "I'm too fat" phase, and on the whole ate better than I did since I was on the road for many meals.

When Danielle hung up after talking to her friend, I remarked, "Your friend didn't sound convinced."

Danielle said, "His mom fixes the meal, and the family all sits down together every night. But he is gay and hasn't told his parents because he knows that they wouldn't understand."

So much for the closeness and quality time of family meals.

MIND'S EYE

A few months into the transition, a close friend was visiting when Danielle came exuberantly through the living room in her girlish teenage manner.

After she was gone, I asked my friend, "Isn't she just the cutest thing?"

His answer echoed in my ears for days. "In my mind's eye," he said, "I still see the boy I used to know."

Again and again that phrase went through my head. I had retrained my mind's eye so that now I only saw the girl, but I understood his reaction. In the beginning, even though my real eye could see the girl, my old brain would spit out male pronouns. After that experience, I could better understand why some parents have trouble allowing their children to grow up and change. In their mind they still have the image of a beloved toddler, an innocent seven or eight year-old, or a rebellious teenager. It takes some time for the mind's eye to replace the youthful image with a new picture of the adult.

My friend saw the boy that used to be,
I just saw a jubilant daughter.

This may explain why a husband does not notice a new hairstyle, or why the family doesn't notice grandma's wrinkles. It is even more difficult to replace the old image with one of the opposite gender.

Since I saw Danielle every day, my mind's eye had been retrained until I no longer saw the little boy, but only a lovable teenage girl. It was more difficult for Danielle's relatives to retrain their minds when they saw her infrequently or only in pictures. Even though our eyes had seen the same person, my friend still saw the boy that used to be, whereas I just saw a jubilant daughter.

Crosses

We all have our secrets
and crosses to bear. Some we can see
and some we will never know have been there.

My special daughter was once a son.
You would not know it if you met her.
How many have we met not knowing?

Please don't judge her
by how things are supposed to be
because they are not.

Appreciate the beauty and the irony.
She will not harm you or change you
except to soften your prejudices.

It's hard to imagine how it feels inside,
but everyone has some burden
and the need to be who they are.

PART IV.......FINISHING TOUCHES

Counselor Hunter referred Danielle to an endocrinologist within a few weeks even though the Harry Benjamin Standards of Care recommend three months of counseling before hormones are started. Danielle was well into puberty and time was of the essence. The first endocrinologist did a complete physical and lots of laboratory tests and prescribed the estrogen, Premarin. His charge was $360.00. The doctor owned the lab, and this made me wonder a about conflict of interest. Danielle was thrilled and anxious to get the prescription filled so she could start the estrogen.

It did not work any magic, but she began to have some breast tenderness, and the growth of her facial hair seemed to slow down a little. Her voice had only begun to change, and we hoped the hormones would keep it from getting lower. But there was also a downside to taking hormones. She experienced fatigue, nausea, and emotional ups and downs as she started down the long and rocky road of side effects from hormone therapy. She became hypersensitive to people looking at her, not paranoid, but just very aware that people seemed to notice her. She became anxious even around people who were loving and accepting of her and needed to get away to rest after several hours with them.

During her first check-up, I questioned the endocrinologist about the fatigue, but he didn't think the Premarin had anything to with it. Her testosterone was still not down to an acceptable level, so he prescribed even more Premarin. On the lower dose she was already missing days of school because she was tired and didn't feel good.

After networking with other transgender people, I learned that fatigue is a very common side effect as is clearly reported on the information sheet that comes with the Premarin. They also told me there was another endocrinologist whose prices were better, and he prescribed an androgen blocker, spironolactone, in addition to Premarin.

During her first visit with the new endocrinologist, the doctor asked Danielle why she had come to him, and was very surprised to learn that she was a transsexual. He lowered the dose of estrogen and added spironolactone. He also said he did not think that fatigue was connected to the hormones. His charge for the complete physical and the necessary laboratory tests was $160.

After reading all the books I could find about hormones written by experts, and talking to several others, I came to the conclusion that there are several choices in the treatment of transsexuals, and each has its advantages and disadvantages. It seems that every doctor has his favorite type and amount of estrogen that he prescribes. I was really amazed that the endocrinologists were not aware of the emotional toll that their patients were experiencing because of the estrogen therapy. They do tests for liver damage and heart problems, but they have no way to measure fatigue, depression, and distraction. Our transgender friends had found what worked for them including hormone injections or additional non-prescription hormones from Mexico. Everybody experiences a different degree of benefits and side effects from hormone therapy, and some feel neither fatigue nor depression.

Danielle did her own research and reduced her dose until she could handle the fatigue and emotions, but it was not enough to give her breasts. She finally decided that she would rather buy her breasts from a plastic surgeon and stay on a hormone dose that allowed her to function.

The first therapist (the hippie) we saw about the gender dysphoria made a good impression on me, but Danielle was not yet ready to see a counselor. She felt she had no emotional problems, she just wanted to be a girl. However, we found we had no choice in the matter because we needed a counselor's referral for hormones and later for a recommendation for surgery. Although I would have trusted the first counselor to work with Danielle, we could not waste our time on a therapist who could not refer us to surgery, no matter how nice he was.

After waiting three months with no word from Counselor Hunter, I called to ask him if there was anything else we should be doing. He set up another appointment at which time Danielle reported that she was having unusual fatigue, and cried easily since being on the hormone therapy. He thought she needed Prozac for her depression; he too said hormones would not cause fatigue. I rejected the suggestion of Prozac because of its reputation for treating mental dysfunction, and I was reluctant to add more drugs to her young body. From the questions he asked, it was apparent he had not looked at the information questionnaire we had returned to him (with $150) three months earlier. I couldn't see that we were getting anything that could be called "counseling." We left without any return appointment or any mention of seeing him again.

Danielle wanted surgery, but I needed to know the costs involved, and whether anyone would do Sex Reassignment Surgery on a young transsexual. I wanted a realistic time frame before raising Danielle's hopes.

We found there were only four or five Sex Reassignment surgeons in the U.S. and Canada who were well known. One surgeon would not treat anyone under age 21. Another was not well known in our area, so there was little information. The surgery cost less in Canada, but we heard rumors of post-op complications. This was no time to scrimp because I wanted

70

the best for my daughter. When I talked to post-op transsexuals, Dr. Schrang in Wisconsin was given rave reviews by all his patients, and I learned that he had treated younger patients. We felt it was important to have the operation soon to give Danielle the best chance for adjusting to young adulthood. When we contacted Dr. Schrang and he learned of the circumstances, he said he would be glad to work with Danielle. He named one price that would cover his fee, the hospital stay and all expenses involved with the actual surgery.

I had been without health insurance for years, betting that my children and I would avoid any catastrophic injury or illness. When I learned of the expected expenses of Danielle's hormone therapy and surgery, I inquired about insurance coverage for her needs, even though I knew we'd probably have to wait a year to satisfy a waiting period for pre-existing conditions. Several companies never returned my call. The representative for one company said the expense for hormones could probably be taken care of if the doctor cooperated, but there was no way surgery could be covered.

I applied for Crippled Children Funds through the State of California, and learned that non-necessary medical expenses could not be covered. I talked to the Shriners and several other groups who help with special medical needs for children. They were very polite to me on the phone, but their organizations did not cover this situation. I talked to one group who would only fund medical expenses for children who had a terminal illness. There are "feel good" programs available for teens in an effort to prevent suicide, alcohol and drug abuse, but there were no funds available for my child. Finally, I figured my financial resources would cover the cost of the surgery in the next year or two if I used credit cards for some of the cost.

Now that we knew that surgery was possible, we needed to seriously pursue counseling in order to get our two surgical referral letters.

Since I hadn't heard from Counselor Hunter in six months, I called to set up a third appointment. At that time we discussed the psychological testing that he had previously mentioned at a cost of $700. The tests included:

- MCMI-III (Million Clinical Multiaxial Inventory)
- Bendar Gestalt
- The Draw A Person/Family
- Wechler (IQ)
- TAT (Thematic Apperceptual Test)
- Rorschach
- MMPI (Minnesota Multiphasic Personality Inventory)

I questioned the need for testing since he had written me a note stating that "Danielle seems relatively stabilized all things considered." He said, "There is no pass or fail to the testing. I just have to do it to protect myself against lawsuits. I don't have to defend myself. All my previous associates have gone out of business due to lawsuits. My wife does the testing and it is a real bargain at the $700 price that I am giving you. It would cost twice as much at the University."

Somehow I kept feeling like a victim. He was taking my money and doing no counseling. I appreciated that he did not make us wait for three months of counseling before sending us to an endocrinologist, and he was not wasting our time with many appointments. But we were getting no help from him and he seemed to only want money.

As we learned more about the situation, we learned that we had few choices. If we went to another counselor, the six months of counseling required (at $100 an hour) before surgery would have to begin again. To save time, we might as well pay the $700.00 to Counselor Hunter and get on with it. I called the counselor and undiplomatically told him. "OK. I'm ready to be screwed."

He called back to say, "I really do not want you as a client, but I will send your records to Counselor Bell."

I had previously met Counselor Bell when I attended a transsexual support meeting, which he was conducting with an associate, Counselor Jenny. At that time I had the opportunity to ask if there was anything more that I could be doing for Danielle. They said I was doing very well with Danielle, and had no further advice to give me. When I told them that I felt Counselor Hunter was not doing any counseling, Counselor Bell told me he could not see us unless Mr. Hunter referred Danielle to him because of professional courtesy.

I continued to attend their support meetings and became part of the support system. Counselor Bell suggested that Danielle attend the support meetings in order to meet others like herself. Danielle went only once. She had already met several transsexuals whom I had invited to our home to chat, and she and Laura were fast friends by then.

The counselors discontinued their meetings at the end of the summer, but Danielle continued to see Counselor Bell privately. He was a very quiet, soft-spoken man, and I was well enough acquainted with him to feel comfortable having Danielle see him alone. Danielle told me she had to save up things to talk about during the sessions since the counselor didn't say very much. Danielle always referred to being transsexual as her "situation"; she never called it a problem. After her first session, the counselor told me that Danielle seemed to be doing fine, and he could see no problem with referring her for surgery when the time came. He would also arrange for the second opinion by another associate in his office. Counselor Bell believed the psychological testing was unnecessary.

The date for surgery was finally set, and we had the first surgery referral letter in the bag. Dr. Bell referred us to Counselor Wolf for another letter, but that was not as simple as it sounded. Our encounter with Dr. Wolf is well documented in the two letters that follow:

Tim Wolf, Ph.D.
Individual, Child, Adolescent & Relationship Psychotherapy

April 5, 1996

Mrs. Evelyn

San Diego, Ca. 92109

RE: Danielle

Mrs. .

After my evaluation of Danielle   on 3-15 and 3-29, 1996, I am not refering her for Sexual Reassignment Surgery. Although Danielle may be an excellent candidate for SRS in the future, she does not appear to be developmentally and socially mature for such a decision at this time.

Danielle appears to be experiencing alterations of mood, impulsivity of behavior, social oppositionalism, and peer adjustments. While these may be developmentally appropriate characteristics for her age, they may also cloud judgments about the future.

Danielle was given three subtests of the Wechsler Intelligence Scale to measure her social maturity. The Wechsler is a standardized intelligence test normed with other 17 year olds. Her scores are as follows: Similarities: This is a test of ability to understand abstract concepts, logical thinking, and concept formation. Danielle scores in the average range on this test. Comprehension: This is a test of practical judgment and common sense regarding social situations. Danielle scores in the low average range on this subtest. Picture Arrangement: This is a test of planning ability related to social intelligence. Danielle scores significantly low on this test.

I would recommend Danielle have two years before she makes a decision for SRS.

Sincerely,

Tim Wolf, Ph.D.

cc.

4525 Park Boulevard, Suite 207 • San Diego, CA 92116 • (619) 542-0088

75

Tim Wolf, Ph.D.   7-
23-96
Individual, Child, Adolescent & relationship Psychotherapy
25 Park Boulevard, Suite 207
San Diego, Ca 92116

I need to address several issues with you about teenage
Gender Dysphoria, and my teenager in particular. These are the
facts as Danielle and I perceived them about our encounters
March 15 and March 29.

We were referred to you by Dr. Chris Beletsis for a 2nd
opinion letter for SRS surgery. You quoted a 2 hr. minimum at
$90.00 an hour and $25.00 for a letter. We filled out the
standard consent forms, you said you would be doing some
testing with Danielle, and you said you would contact us to set
up the 2nd appointment.

After the first hour, she said she had talked to you for a few
minutes and then had done some kind-of dumb tests where you
asked her questions about hypothetical situations and also had
her put pictures in order, which she felt could have been
correctly placed in several orders with an explanation.

Since you did not seem to need my input at the first
appointment, she felt she could go by herself to the 2nd
appointment and I would not lose the time from work.

She called me about 4:30 the afternoon after her 2nd
appointment, which did not last even half an hour, to tell me of
her 2nd experience with you. She wisely waited until my
workday was almost over because she knew I would be upset.
She said that you told her that you did not believe that anyone
under 21 should have SRS surgery, but if they tested above
average you might consider it. You then told her that her scores
showed that she was below average intelligence.

I called and asked you for a written summary of your
evaluation of Danielle, which you sent. In the letter you said
"Danielle appears to be experiencing alterations of mood,

impulsivity of behavior, social oppositionalism and peer adjustments." And you recommended that she wait 2 years before making a decision on SRS surgery.

Danielle has had a learning disability that we have been dealing with for many years. I have worked very hard to maintain a positive self-esteem about her intelligence. Her two older brothers have always done really well academically and she felt bad because she could not keep up with them. I always emphasized other talents that she has. Since her transition, she has progressed amazingly in her academic abilities and had been feeling really good about herself. You telling her that she was below average intelligence crushed her. She was very discouraged at the thought of facing another 2-4 years of having to tuck her penis, of having to take the mega doses of hormones, that she herself knows alter her moods and makes her physically nauseated. The thought of not being able to date as her peers are doing. The fear of being discovered. A teenager with any less maturity might have thought of ending her life.

1. You knew she was 17 when we came to you. You should have been honest with us about your apparent preconceived belief that anyone under 21 should not have surgery

2. I thought you were going to base your decision on an interview with her, not on standardized testing. I did not know there was a pass/fail situation with standardized testing.

3. I thought you understood that people on mega hormones, are emotional and impulsive. It is the equivalent to PMS or worse.

4. If you had talked with me at all, you would have understood that she gets her social oppositionalism from me. Which is one of the reasons that she is doing so well in the situation that she is in. I have always promoted being an individual, questioning authority, not paying any attention to what others might think.

5. You should never have told a teenager who is struggling with so many other issues that she is below average intelligence. That to me is unforgivable, especially when you are supposedly an expert on adolescent and relationship psychotherapy. I am sorry that I exposed my teenager to you. You did more harm than good. Several times since she met with you she has asked me for reassurance that she really is intelligent. Shame on you.

6. If you had taken the time to know her at all personally, instead of basing your opinion on testing, you would have understood that she is doing really well under the circumstances. She attends a regular high-school full time with a B average. She is not on drugs, does not smoke, or drink. She has a job doing peer counseling through "Planned Parenthood". I often have to be out of town overnight and she is responsible enough to be left alone without getting into trouble. I feel she is wise beyond her years in the insights she expresses in dealing with her situation and the real world around her. (Not hypothetical situations.)

7. My daughter and I are well known and respected in the gender community and our opinions matter. A copy of this letter will be widely distributed. Your name will go on the list of those that take advantage of our community and are enriching themselves at our expense.

* * * * *

He never responded to my letter.

When I complained to the State Medical Board about Dr. Wolf, I learned that he had completed the education for his Ph.D., but was not licensed to practice psychology with that degree.

The Harry Benjamin Standard of Care Guidelines says that a therapist familiar with the program and the transsexual will be able to help during the process. In Danielle's case, we found that most of the therapists seemed to be there to impede progress rather than to assist. The counselors, who admitted they had very little experience with teen transsexuals, were still willing to charge like *experts*. None of the counselors seemed to care what I thought and tried to ignore me, maybe hoping I would go away.

The date for surgery was quickly approaching, and the situation was getting desperate. We still did not have a second referral letter, and I never, ever wanted to see another counselor, but we had no choice.

In tears, I shared Dr. Wolf's letter with Counselor Jenny. She and I had been speakers at the educational outreach speakers' bureau on several occasions, and we once investigated an alternative school for Danielle in another city together, so she knew both Danielle and me. She carefully considered the matter, and decided that she could probably write a letter for surgery although she had never written one before. We were relieved when she wrote the second opinion letter for us after only one session with Danielle.

There were other counselors in our community. One believed in the Nurture theory - absent father, domineering mother, or a mother who really wanted a girl - with which I disagreed. She believed that transsexuals are all homosexuals who cannot deal with being gay. This is an outdated theory for it is now understood that sexual orientation and gender identity are two entirely different issues. Some transsexuals look for a partner of the same sex as they are after surgery. Some counselors believe that Gender Dysphoria is usually just a phase when it occurs in younger children. I wonder if it is just a phase or do children learn very quickly to hide feelings that others disapprove of.

In this world, there must be some good counselors who really care and help the transsexual community deal with their issues. Because the HBIGDA *(WPATH)* Standards of Care require counseling in preparation for surgery, the transsexuals become pawns in the conflict of interest game. The Standards are maintained and continue to be revised by professionals who are qualified to do the counseling and who stand to gain financially. Although counseling before an important decision such as Sex Reassignment surgery could be beneficial, it would also be beneficial before marriage and having children. The benefits of counseling are questionable because transsexuals soon learn to give answers that the counselor wants to hear.

I hope to see the HBIGDA *(WPATH)* Standards changed in the future to take into account that some transsexuals (and perhaps most) are not psychologically unbalanced. If transsexuals are psychologically handicapped they probably would not be able to get enough money together for surgery. There is no proof that a transsexual with perceived psychological problems would be worse off for having surgery.

Recently I have had some correspondence with therapist Jude Patton who said, "I am not at all like the other therapists you encountered, nor are many other experienced therapists who deal with gender issues. I may have an advantage in empathy, because I am both a professional AND a peer. (I am female to male, post-op transsexual for over 25 years.) My own care givers certainly 'bent the rules' to get me the care I needed at the time, and I've never forgotten it."

He explained, "Each client should be the 'Captain of their own ship' with the therapist acting as a 'Navigator.' Not a gatekeeper, but a guide, educator, support system and advocate. The treatment goals should be a joint effort of client and therapist with the client a full partner in the planning of the treatment."

I fully concur with that philosophy, and I believe that there are some who do not need emotional therapy during the gender transition process, especially if they have supportive family and friends.

Harry Benjamin Standards of Care

A friend loaned me a videotape showing the sex reassignment procedure planned by Dr. Schrang. I told Danielle that it was available, but doubted she would want to see it, but I was wrong - she was very much interested. It was I who was not anxious to know the details of the surgery, but I felt that I should watch with her in case she had any questions. When we played the video, she became totally engrossed, and even rewound the film to watch several segments a second time to be sure she understood everything. I was not impressed by the after pictures that showed the final results, but Danielle commented, "Everything was so neat and tidy afterwards. All the stuff is gone."

Then Dr. Schrang presented another obstacle. He would not operate on Danielle without the signed consent of both parents, or from a parent who had sole custody. My marriage and divorce had both taken place in Mexico where the subject of custody was never addressed. Danielle had lived with me since she was two years old and I had paid the bills, so I figured she was mine. "Possession is nine-tenths of the law." I sought the advice of a lawyer friend concerning the cost and ramifications of getting a legal custody order. With such an order, perhaps I could collect child support for all the past years although realistically there was little hope of getting financial assistance from her father now any more than it was in the past. I learned that the sole custody order, even if not protested would probably cost $400 or more.

Having her father sign the permission for surgery would be the best way, but not necessarily the easiest since he was still upset because his son was living as a girl. Without much hope, I called him to give it a try. When he refused to sign, I begged, threatened, and tried every angle

"I will go to court and get sole custody," I said, "But it will cost me some money."

He said, "I will contest the court order."

"That will be fine with me, because then the judge will make you pay child support for all the past years when you have paid nothing."

If he thought he deserved to have a vote about Danielle's future, he would have to pay for the privilege. The next day he called to say that he was ready to sign the papers, and I arranged to meet him right away at a Notary Public's office before he changed his mind. With her father's signature in hand, Danielle and I had passed a huge milestone.

We scheduled the surgery for early summer 1996, between her junior and senior years in high school when she would be 17 1/2 years old. Two years would have passed between the time that I found out she was transsexual and the time of surgery, and I presumed we would have finished the required counseling.

Danielle had a steady boyfriend at the end of her second year of high school as we prepared for surgery. He often spent time at our house because life with his own family was apparently difficult. It was all right with me because I liked the young man. He took her to the prom, and even spent the night several times at our home. As we made arrangements to go to Wisconsin for surgery, she finally told him about herself. She could not lie to him about why she was going to be gone for two weeks and then recuperating for several more. He was quiet and withdrawn for a long time, and then commented that it only made her more interesting to him.

When she told another boy she had dated, he quit dating her in a romantic sense but continued being her pal and friend. Some boys lost interest in her because she was prudish and did not allow much touching. She never encountered violence because she was transsexual, although she had to run away from a situation in Mexico because a guy thought he could have his way with this young girl.

I had to work extra-long hours before we went to Wisconsin in order to be away for the two weeks required for surgery. I could feel the stress taking its toll as we made our last preparations. Danielle was getting excited as the time drew near, but seemed quite calm. However, during the last two weeks before leaving, she had several anxiety attacks. I kept searching my soul, wondering if this surgery was the right thing to do.

During our flight to Wisconsin, I thought of the serious consequences of our trip. The others on the plane had no idea that this beautiful teen girl was on her way to a hospital for very complicated surgery in order to gain inner peace. I wondered what other parents would think of me for facilitating the sex reassignment surgery. There could be complications, and I worried about that, too. I was on the verge of tears the whole way, but did not want Danielle to know that I was stressed out. It would be wrong for me to add to any anxiety that she might have already. Danielle appeared to be calm, but I learned later that she had tried to keep me from knowing of her anxiety.

We landed at the huge airport in Minneapolis/St. Paul with only a few minutes to make connections for our flight to Appleton. As we left the plane, the stewardess directed us to our departure gate at the other end of the airport. Danielle went ahead to get us checked in because she could get there faster than I. When I caught up with her she had bad news - the gate we wanted was actually back where we had come from, close to our arrival gate. I knew it was too late to get there, but Danielle went ahead again to make the arrangements in case the plane was late. The thoughts that went through my mind are not fit to print. Why does it have to be so difficult to change planes? I condemned the airlines and lots of other people and things as I went cussing and crying the long way back to where we started.

As I had feared, when we arrived at the proper gate, we had missed the plane. I lay down on a bench and fell apart. I told Danielle that I just couldn't do it - I was going home. She chased off the solicitous airport personnel, calmed me down, and went to get tickets for a later flight and then to eat and look at the airport gift shops.

My family and many of my acquaintances had admired me for maintaining a calm and reasonable attitude through this whole gender change situation. I was glad that they couldn't see me in a puddle of tears in the airport. Although I knew I had been under a lot of stress, I had not realized the extent of it. One of my mottoes is "Lie down and cry awhile, then pick up the pieces and go on." This stress management system had worked before and it did this time too. After a good cry, I pulled myself together and we went on to Appleton.

Once in our rental car, it was not difficult to locate the doctor's office, hospital, shopping center, and motel in the small city. After we were settled in, we went to a local restaurant for Danielle's last meal before surgery.

When we met Dr. Schrang in his office the next morning, he was very pleasant. He appropriately addressed Danielle as she was the patient, almost ignoring me. He emphasized that the proposed operation would not change the way the world would treat her, nor magically change her life, nor solve all her problems. Danielle must carefully follow all the post-op instructions, and take responsibility for her "aftercare". He could do the surgery, but it was up to her to make the outcome successful.

After checking into the hospital, we toured the floor where the sex reassignment patients were housed. At one end of the hall was a sitting room overlooking the Fox River - a peaceful area that became my favorite spot. We met Danielle's roommate, Gloria who had just returned from surgery, and her very attentive wife. They were impressed with Danielle's youth and beauty. During the next ten days we became quite close to them as they encouraged and helped us. We discovered that most of the transsexuals on the surgical ward were alone with no one to support them during their ordeal.

Danielle appeared to be calm and unafraid throughout the necessary preparations that evening and the next morning, and she went off to surgery having never expressed fear, but only looking forward to the future.

* * * * *

(I had planned to give this poem/prayer to the surgeon but lost my courage.)

Bless You

May you be blessed as you correct the errant ways of Mother Nature.

May your hands be steady as you do your artwork that may be seen by few.

May your eyes be clear as you put finishing touches on our dear one's life.
May your mind be sharp as you make your masterpiece decisions.

Bless you as you care for those misunderstood by many and loved by few.

* * * * *

Accounts of the step-by-step process of the actual surgery are available from other sources, so I will not include that technical information here.

My Mom arrived while Danielle was still in surgery, and we talked and put together a jigsaw puzzle in the waiting room to pass the time. I had brought the jigsaw puzzle with me because I knew I would not be able to concentrate on reading, and making puzzles has always been a very calming and restful pastime for me. My mind was with Danielle and what they were doing to her, but the die was cast, and now we just had to deal with the results of our decisions.

She was returned to her room, and as she came out of the fog of general anesthesia, she asked me, "Is it all over?"

When I said, "Yes," she smiled from ear to ear. She looked very pale, and the sight of so many attached tubes and wires was distressing to me, and I started crying, for a mother suffers too when her child is in pain. Still I knew that this pain was temporary and far better than the mental anguish and misery of soul that she had suffered during the years she was locked inside the wrong body. Gloria's wife and others thought I was crying at the finality of no longer having my son. They reassured me that my son was not gone, but was still there as a new and happier person, but I had already accepted this new person, and had almost forgotten that she was ever anything but a wonderful daughter.

The next few days were pretty rough for both of us. I thought that I could sit and write a lot of this book while she slept, but there was not much time for rest because she needed help with so many little things. There were many phone calls from well wishers and flowers from our friends in California and elsewhere.

We even received a call from a young transsexual in Australia whom we had met on the Internet, and who would soon be having surgery. Danielle did not seem to comprehend the tremendous outpour of love and hope for her. I felt as if she was the poster child of the transsexual community. Danielle had an opportunity that many could only dream about - the support of her family, and surgery when she was young. All those advantages were not lost on Danielle, for she repeatedly expressed her gratitude to me, and her thankfulness that she had been able to go through the surgery.

Her grandmother stayed two days after the surgery and gave Danielle a cuddly Teddy bear, which seemed to give her some comfort.

She grinned from ear to ear

Danielle's roommate Gloria wrote a poem for her:

Today We Are Butterflies

We have traveled our respective roads as caterpillars, we consumed all of the information we could about our confused lives and we learned and we grew.

Finally our roads that we have traveled have joined for our final journey. We've spun our cocoons and with much nurturing and love we entered the pupa stage. And through the hands   of   a skilled Doctor we were able to break out of our pupal bonds and
at last we were born to live the lives we were meant to live.

As we dry our wings and prepare to go forth in our new lives as beautiful butterflies we pause to give thanks.

* . * . * . * . *

Danielle suffered from post-op vomiting which was not serious, and she lost enough blood over the next few days that she had to be given three units by transfusion. Although many people offered to donate blood, the facility did not participate in a donor program; however the cost of the transfusion was small. Dr. Schrang did things very quickly without explaining them to Danielle beforehand. He didn't say more than two words to me the whole nine days we were there. I had the feeling that we were nameless, faceless bodies to him. He came and went so quickly, we joked that the only reason we knew he had been there was the lingering sent of his cologne. The nurses were very attentive and we appreciated their help.

When we returned to the motel, one of only two in town, Danielle started the process of the frequent dilating of the new vagina following the doctor's instruction meticulously. It would have been almost impossible for Danielle to have managed alone. Going out to get supplies and finding food that Danielle felt like eating kept me busy. Since Danielle had to stay flat in bed for seven days in the hospital, it took several days to get the tangles out of her hair. After a while, I began to suffer from cabin fever. Following our return visit to the doctor, we were both glad to be heading for home.

The trip home was long and exhausting. Danielle's boyfriend met us at the airport to help get her home and situated. Danielle was too tired to do the dilating that night and wanted to give up completely, but after a good night's rest she was ready to go on with the demanding schedule. During the next few weeks her time was spent taking care of herself according to the instructions she was given. She could only leave the house for an hour or so between treatments, and when her boyfriend and others came to visit she had little time to spend with them because she had to be back in her room dilating. There was an infection at the site where a tight wire suture had been, and she still has a scar in that area, which is now pretty well covered by pubic hair. Scars on the skin donor sites on the hips on both sides were much bigger than I had expected, but she didn't seem to mind. I was pleased by the visual results of the vaginal surgery at least from a casual glance. Danielle frequently paraded around the house in the buff or close to it in order to enjoy the way she felt without all the "stuff" down there. Another surgery (labiaplasty) would be necessary at some future date to give the finishing cosmetic touches to the genital area.

After a month of dilating, Danielle was supposed to graduate to a larger circumference dilator. The surgeon had given us a brochure that offered five dilators in graduating dimensions for $90.00. These dilators were solid and did not vibrate, and two of them were smaller than needed. Since I knew that I could buy many types and shapes of dilators at the adult bookstore in our area, we did not buy the expensive set. After buying two different vibrators that did not meet Danielle's desires in shape or color or size or something, I gave up in frustration and told her I just didn't understand what she wanted. She said she would go buy what she had in mind. She was only 17 and not allowed in such stores, but she set off anyway with the admonition from me not to give my name if she got caught. She dressed in her best looking "mature" outfit and went on her mission. At the store she found what she wanted and asked the cashier if he knew the circumference of the dilator that she had chosen to make sure that it was bigger than what she already had at home. He went to check the catalogue and came back to announce in a loud voice across the store, "It's one size fits all." She paid for her purchase and no one asked her age or for her ID. I was 40 before I was brave enough to go into an adult store.

* * * * *

In Canada both surgeries are done during one procedure and they do not need to use donor skin. Laura had her surgery later there with a quicker recovery, a less vigorous dilating schedule, and great results. Some of our community have gone to Oregon recently with good results. Dr. Schrang required the longest time in bed, and the most rigorous dilating schedule, but the results from other surgeons seem be just as satisfactory. Both Canada and Oregon have residential facilities for post-surgery care, which is an important consideration for someone going alone.

All the transsexuals that I have met are so thankful for the surgery that they rave about the wonderful experience and are happy with the results. They quickly forget about any complications or unpleasantness accompanying the experience. I call it the "Savior Syndrome." They put the surgeon on a pedestal and are not always objective when asked about their surgery experience.

I made the best choice I could with the information I had at the time, but if I had it to do over again, I might come up with different results. Surgeons are always trying to improve their performance based on more advanced knowledge, and by experimenting with different techniques.

Danielle's hormone therapy continued to cause her mental and emotional ups and downs that were very distressing. We did everything we could to try to stabilize her emotions including a good diet, lots of rest, a positive attitude and natural remedies. Finally, after nothing else seemed to help and after much research, I encouraged her to try Prozac even though we had not wanted to use it before, believing the myth that people who take Prozac are crazy. It has helped her by taking the edge off her anxiety and her feelings of being overwhelmed.

At Christmas, Danielle and I went to visit Ben. He was now a sophomore at a Flagstaff college and was sharing a three-bedroom condo with another young man. Danielle and Ben enjoyed being together while skiing, shopping, and watching movies during the short vacation. Her big brother was gallant, protective, and proud of his sister. They conspired together and came up with a plan. Danielle should move to Flagstaff to get a new start where no one knew her, and Ben thought it would be nice to have her as his third roommate. He didn't admit it, but he was probably a little lonely for some of his family.

Although I looked forward to the time when the children would all be grown so I could regain some freedom and privacy in my life, I was not ready for it right NOW. But I could see the excitement and adventure in their eyes, and after much discussion, I decided I must not let my feelings slow my children's quest for happiness and a future. It was heart-warming for me to see a new bond developing between them.

I knew in my heart that this would be a positive move for Danielle as she had just turned 18 and was exhibiting many nesting instincts.

If she could cook and clean for these boys, it might postpone the time when she would fall into housekeeping with a boyfriend. She and her previous boyfriend had parted ways when she became busy with high school and he had gone on to college. There was another compelling reason for her move. My frequent activist efforts in the transgender community gave her little chance to forget the ordeal that she had been through as she settled into her new life as a girl. I had seen other transgender females leave the community after surgery to blend into society and get on with their lives as women. After all, being able to live as a teenage girl was the purpose for Danielle's surgery.

Soon after we returned home from Christmas vacation, Danielle packed all her belongings into her pickup truck - a television, her bicycle, her feminine bed, many of our kitchen supplies, a large garbage bag full of shoes (a true female) and more stuff than she could possibly need.

"You can come home anytime you want," I told her, "but you can only bring one suitcase."

Danielle disappeared like a nomad into the desert with her truck full of everything she owned. She called me several times along the road but forgot to call when she arrived safely. That was a very long day for me and my seldom-used apron strings. At first I called every day, but was gradually weaned as it became harder and harder to catch her at home between high school and social activities. Danielle was gone for now, and I moved into a small studio apartment.

You can only bring home one suitcase.

Since she had to take such low doses of hormones due to the emotions, she did not develop much breast growth. At 18 she still was not endowed enough to notice. Some think breasts will come if you wait long enough. Some are sure there is some magic combination of hormones that produce breasts. There are those who think flat is OK, but Danielle really wanted breasts. I remember how much I had wanted breasts as a teenager, but I did not get them until I started having children. Since that was not an option for Danielle, we decided to go ahead with breast implants during the next summer. She made all the arrangements for surgery after consulting with several plastic surgeons in Phoenix. One surgeon required a current psychological evaluation. I thought that was unfair since anybody else can have breast enlargement surgery on demand. Some women probably need counseling to discover why huge breasts are important to them. Why should transsexuals be presumed to be unbalanced just because they want breasts?

I went to Phoenix to be with her before and after surgery. Again she was very brave - she never complained. As she was coming out of the anesthetic, she said amusing things. "Be quiet. You are talking too loud. Don't touch me. I don't want my breasts anymore because they hurt." Then she apologized for being rude. I didn't know why she thought she was being rude, but later she said she was sorry that she told us to be quiet and leave her alone.

The surgery was done on an outpatient basis, so we returned to our motel in Phoenix a few hours after it was completed. The next two days in the motel were very long and uncomfortable for her because she had trouble keeping food and liquids down, yet she needed to eat something when she took the pills to relieve the severe pain. Every time she wanted to move, I had to help her change position, and rearrange the ice pack on her new breasts to keep the swelling down. I only slept for an hour or so at a time. Her brother had volunteered to take care of her after surgery, but I was glad that I was there even though she needed more attention than I had anticipated. But we did it.

Now she is happy with her body that matches her mind, and I am happy that we were able to do all the things to make her whole.

Danielle continued to live in Flagstaff with Ben and started her senior year there. One day my pager showed an Arizona area code but I did not recognize the number. Police, hospital, accident, flashed through my mind as I dialed the number. It was Danielle's high school, and the vice-principal wanted to talk with me.

"Is this Danielle's mother?" he asked.

"Yes."

"I just want to confirm something that Danielle said in class today."

"Yes." I waited expectantly.

"Today she told her class that she has had sex reassignment surgery."

"Ohhhh shit!!"

"Well," he said with a chuckle. "I guess that confirms it."

"Do you know how this came about?"

He said, "There have been rumors and Danielle evidently felt the time was right to let people know about her past so they could get over it and quit whispering."

"I wish she hadn't told everyone," I said.

"She has a right to tell. She has a right to be safe at this school and finish her high school here. We like her very much, and are going to help her in any way we can. We will guard her confidentiality if any press or other parents inquire about her. We are going to make sure she is not made fun of or harassed here on campus. I have already talked to her about not isolating herself. Do you think she is strong enough to handle this?"

"Some days she is stronger than others," I said with all honesty. "I'll call and talk to her."

I thanked him profusely for his understanding and help, and said I would get back to him. My stomach was churning. Would she ever be able to get away from her past? Had the move to Flagstaff been in vain? If she had to move again, there was still David in San Jose. He had moved there for a good job after graduating from college, the same year Ben graduated from high school.

After the vice-principal called me, any hope of concentrating on job for the day was gone, so I called Danielle right away. She said she had not called me because she didn't want to worry me. "Anyway," she assured me, "it's no big deal."

She told me more about the circumstances leading up to her revelation. She had recently become aware of rumors about her. One girl had asked her if she had had sex reassignment surgery. Danielle countered with, "That's a stupid question to ask anyone." For a sociology class assignment she wrote an autobiography, but without revealing the truth, she knew it made no sense. She was sad that she could not reveal her real self, especially when she received a D on the paper. After much consideration, and all on her own, she decided to ask permission from a substitute teacher to make an announcement near the end of the class period. It was then she told her story to her classmates and the teacher, then left immediately since it was near the end of the school day.

Within five minutes the story had spread through the whole school.

As soon as the principal and vice-principal heard, they visited her at home to see that she was all right and was not alone. Ben was already there because one of Danielle's friends had called to warn him that Danielle might need him. The school representatives talked with Ben and Danielle for some time, then returned to the school, at which time the vice-principal called me. Even after talking to the kids, he could not quite believe that Danielle had once been a boy

While she was telling me about all that had taken place, she kept reassuring me. "It's no big deal, everything is going to be fine, so just don't worry."

"I'm your mother, that's my job."

I wanted to get in the car, drive eight hours to Flagstaff and bring her home to safety, but I realized that I could not give her safety anywhere. She had to work through this for herself. She could either be brave and proud by sticking it out or move to another new place and keep her mouth shut, thus denying part of who she is.

When I called a friend for support, he said, "You should be proud of her. She is turning out to be an activist just like her mother", and I didn't expect any less of her, for I have seen in her the courage and determination to be herself.

I called the vice-principal the next day to tell him that Danielle thought everything was going to be fine. I learned that he had a meeting with Danielle's teachers to let them know about the situation and to request their help in assuring that she was not made fun of nor harassed in any way.

He did have a question. "Is her surgery complete so I can say that she is legally a female?"

That was an important question since she was in a girl's gym class. I assured him that she was legally a female. I also told him I would send him a packet of information about transsexuals.

I said, "Be proud of her for me."

He added, "We are all proud of her."

The next day I watched the clock while trying to keep my mind on my work until I could call Danielle after her first day "out" at school. She told me, "My day went really well. People gave me notes and letters of support. One girl even brought me flowers! Total strangers came up to me to say how brave I was. They call me by name, but I don't know who they are."

A week later I called the vice-principal again to see if he had survived. He told me, "There has been no press, no parents, no problems. Danielle seems to be doing fine. No big deal. I warned the principals of the two other high schools in town to confirm with me any rumors they might hear about this high school, but they haven't heard a thing."

He thanked me for the packet of information on transsexuals, which he had passed on to his administrative superiors and to his staff. We both agreed that this was a tremendous learning experience for students and staff. I thanked him again for his care and understanding. The high school had handled the situation in a very exemplary manner. Finally I had found a school representative that was truly concerned about and considerate of his students' needs.

The Mexican American Club voted Danielle their president. A boy she had dated came to her house to watch movies again even though he knew about her past. Danielle kept telling me, "It's no big deal, nobody cares." I wanted to tell her it was a very big deal. It may have seemed like a small step for her, but it was a big step towards the better understanding of those with gender dysphoria.

* . * . * . * . *

The subject of transsexualism is misunderstood by the general population whose thinking is still in the dark ages. I was born an activist and now I have a cause.

My local school district has a committee to deal with gay and lesbian issues and to educate teaching staff about methods of protecting students from discrimination. The organization Parents and Friends of Lesbians and Gays (PFLAG) needed a representative on this committee and I volunteered. At one of the first meetings I met Ellen, the school district employee who had talked to me when I was trying to learn the school district's policy on transsexuals. The only information she would gave me at that time was, "we do not discriminate." As I suspected at the time, she was instructed by a supervisor to say nothing else. Ellen told me that she felt terrible that she had not been allowed to be more helpful, and was very glad to know that we had found a safe school for Danielle.

I joined the team that talks to teachers in elementary and high schools in our district about treating all students the same and making school a safe place for everyone. I share with them the instances when teachers and counselors did not know what to do with Daniel. My goal is simply to let every teacher at least hear the word transsexual. My hope is that in the future every school will be a safe place for Danielle and others like her. We leave written information at the school that includes resources and people to contact for more information.

Teachers in many of the schools have already seen students with gender issues. Although there still is not much that a teacher can do, they can at least be accepting and try to protect the student from teasing and ridicule. Unless the parents are involved in the student's situation, the teachers' hands are tied.

International Conference on Transgender Law & Employment Policy, Inc. (ICTLEP) is a group of lawyers & professionals working on the legal and employment issues for transsexuals. I attended one of their annual meetings in Texas and found it very interesting, although most of the subjects addressed concerned transgender adults: employment, child custody, marriage, legal papers, etc. There seemed to be no one dealing with matters important to teens and students. Again I was impressed by the transsexuals, who were well adjusted working professionals, as well as the movers and shakers in the transgender movement. Although Danielle just wanted to be a girl, there are those who want to be androgynous, or bi-gendered, (sometimes male, sometimes female), or want to establish a third sex or five sexes, or to do away with gender altogether. I learned about the intersexed or hermaphrodites and their quest to choose their own gender, and not have some surgeon decide at birth.

As I became more involved with Neutral Corner, I joined their Speakers Bureau, talking to students at various college classes. One or two transsexuals or crossdressers and I would show these students that the transgender population is human, and won't hurt anyone. Students are in college to be educated and we want to add to their education. We want people to understand that gender identity is not a choice. Who would choose to have such a difficult life? We emphasize that this is not a mental illness.

Unfortunately it is in the best interest of the counseling industry to perpetuate the myth that it is a mental or psychological problem. There are support groups for the transgender individuals so they won't give up and hurt themselves through drug or alcohol abuse or in drastic cases, by suicide.

The national PFLAG organization has invited me to speak several times to help educate their members. At present there are few parents who understand the problems, but we hope that there will be more in the future.

Everywhere I go and tell the story of Danielle and her need to be a girl, someone tells me "You are such a wonderful mother." That statement still surprises me because I have always felt that I was not particularly good at mothering, being a rather unconventional and haphazard parent. I have only done what any mother can do, give unconditional love to my child.

When transsexuals hear my story they tell me that they knew they were transsexuals when they were teenagers, but were afraid to tell their parents. As I became better at using the computer and the Internet, I joined several list servers dealing with transsexualism. There is now a group of parents ready and willing to contact other parents through the Internet. There are also a few teen stories and other relevant information available through these means.

There seems to be an increasing number of younger children telling their parents that they feel they need to be the opposite gender. I hope we can spread the knowledge that these children need love and understanding.

When Danielle was living at home I always told her where I was going to speak and invited her to come with me. She went with me once or twice but was not comfortable talking about her situation in public, or she had other things to do that were more important to a teenager. I respected her wishes not to talk at her school, and she understood my need to try to change the world.

LETTERS FROM FAMILY

We have a family e-mail list including an extended family. The following are two letters written about Danielle for all the family to read. The first is from her brother, and the second from her Grandma Clela. The third letter is from Danielle to the rest of the family.

I.

Hello again everyone.

This is a subject that probably a lot of people have discussed but are a little afraid to ask questions about. The subject I am talking about is my wonderful sister Danielle.

Danielle decided to come clean to me with her secret while she was in Phoenix visiting me. I went to work one day and said good-bye to Daniel and came home to Danielle. At first I was full of self-pity, and didn't know what I was going to do or what everyone would think of it. For several weeks I could hardly sleep at night thinking of what would happen to her and why this had happened to our family. We had already been through so much and now this. Before this happened to our family I had watched talk shows where there were people in similar situations and I had to turn the channel because it made me almost ill. I always thought to myself that the people that were like that must have grown up in some really messed up families. I have since changed my mind and look at all people in a different light.

It's kind of strange how things can change 180 degrees when they hit close to home. At first I really thought no good could possibly come of this change that Daniel had made. He was my brother for 16 years, 16 years is a long time to know someone and then all of a sudden for them to change. The neighbor girl who was a very close friend helped Danielle go through this transformation and they became very close. I had known the neighbor, Denise, for about two years and we were pretty good friends. She helped me to understand a little about why Danielle had done this, and was there to talk to about it when I needed her. It almost felt a little like it was my fault that this had happened because I had been there almost all the time and I let this happen. I tried to think of where it could have gone wrong and why this terrible thing had happened to us.

As time passed, I got more comfortable with it and eventually even got to the point where I could call her Danielle right to her face. I visited my Mom several months ago and took Danielle to the beach to stroll around the boardwalk.

I enjoyed the time I had with her immensely and know that it would have never been nearly the same if I had taken her before she went through the transformation. She had turned from a sort of mischievous boy into the most wonderful girl anyone could know. My friend in Phoenix saw her at graduation and instantly fell in love with her and her lovely smile.

It now seems to me that she is very happy to be alive and transmits that attitude to everyone she knows. I know from stories my Mom tells me that she is very outgoing and meets new people every day. Whenever I call, she is very excited about all kinds of things that she is doing in her life and it just fills my heart with pride because I can see the big smile on her face and know the hard work and struggle she had to deal with to get to where she is. I know if you all knew her the way she is now you would instantly be overwhelmed by the beaming attitude she has toward life, and the courage and confidence she has in herself to be a good person no matter what has happened.

Although at first I felt sorry for myself, I now consider myself lucky to have a sister such as she is. Most people fight with their sisters and don't appreciate them much. I think of how proud I am of mine and know that this is one of the bravest and most warm people I know, and it just so happens that she is my sister. While most girls her age are worried about makeup and perfume and how they won't live without a certain outfit, my sister is enjoying life and bringing joy to those that know her. She has grown up brave just like my Mom and she will be unstoppable in whatever goals she sets for herself and I will stand behind her no matter what she decides.

This brings me to another subject I have to talk about. Some of you may wonder why I am not married and do not really have any serious girlfriends in my life so far. Well, any girl that I meet and is a candidate has some very high expectations from me because two of the women that I admire the most happen to be my family members. That is my Mom and my sister and it will be hard for any girls to come up to par against them. But then, half the fun is finding that special girl that I know has to be out there somewhere.

Love,
David

II. RE: MY NEW GRANDDAUGHTER

David did well to introduce us to his sister, Danielle. I used to have eight grandsons and two granddaughters and now I have seven grandsons and three granddaughters, and the most recent is the oldest. That might be difficult to explain, but not after you have met Danielle.

It has been a little more than a year since Evelyn told me that her 15-year old son, Daniel, had revealed to her that he believed he was really a girl. Almost immediately I said, "He has always been a girl!"

You see, I have many memories of this special child. I remember a small boy of about three years who often sat on the arm of the couch combing and arranging his mother's long and curly hair. (He was still styling her hair years later.) That small boy liked to play with dolls and he saw some kind of value in a dismembered Barbie doll in the toys that I kept for visiting children. On his ninth birthday, his wish was for a doll with long hair and a pony with a long mane - and the family fulfilled his wish. Several times he had me help him make clothes for his doll. He would pick out some material from the scrap box and together we would fashion clothes. His choice of cloth was always the bright shiny pieces.

In kindergarten when he was getting settled in a new school, I asked how he liked it. He said, "It is beautiful! The colors are so pretty." I didn't understand that statement until I had an occasion to pick him up from school. Every schoolroom door around the big court was painted a different color - pink, purple, green, blue, yellow - so it was very colorful. He always described textures, as well as colors, whenever it was appropriate.

He never played any sports, except when he was involved in acrobatic classes, which seemed to fit him naturally. He did exceptionally well with it.

This little grandson was extremely loving. I always got a big hug when he came to visit, another when he left, and usually a time or two during the stay. He was also very sensitive to other people's feelings.

He could tell when someone was not feeling well or was angry or uncomfortable.

At an age when most little boys were finding their best friends from among the boys, his friends were girls. When he had a chance to take two or three friends on an outing on his birthdays, he always picked girls, and this pattern of having girls for his close friends continued through junior high school.

Daniel was always close to his mother in ways that you would not expect of a son. They appeared to have such fun together. When he became old enough to be aware of his mother's clothes, he would advise her on what to wear, and later she always took him along to pick out new clothes for her wardrobe. Two years ago his mother and I helped to host a bridal shower for a friend. Her son, then 13 years old, arranged her hair. He used a small chignon of curls on the back of her hair and with a ribbon, blended it in with her own curls. The style was perfect with the flower print and lace of her dress. She was pretty as a picture, and Daniel appreciated and praised her beauty profusely.

He was the one in the family that would get the urge to clean and straighten the house, and would get after his brothers to put things away. As he started to think about his life work, he chose interior decorating. At one time I sent him a subscription to an interior decorating magazine, and I knew he liked to visit model homes to look at the furnishings.

Those of us close to this special child recognized that he was different, but had no clue as to the cause. He was very animated as he talked, with unusual movements of his hands and body. As I watched him walk, I sometimes thought, "Can't he walk like a boy? Doesn't he know he walks like a girl?" He knew, because his schoolmates teased him about his walk, and I know now that he couldn't do anything about it. Now we see those same movements and animation and feminine gait as perfect for a teenage girl.

The age at which Danielle made this drastic change was unusual, for more often it is made much later in life. It wasn't a sudden idea, for Evelyn knew some months before the announcement that Daniel was emotionally upset. Some have wondered if a teenager of 16 years should be making this important decision. Consider this question: At what point in life did you make the "decision" to be male or female?

Many studies have been done to determine why girls act like girls and boys like boys. From what I have read, it is not because people expect girls to act like girls, but simply because that behavior is genetically determined. Girls play with dolls, are nurturing, and place great importance on relationships. Boys play with cars and trucks, are competitive, and play ball. For more information read, 'Brain Sex' by Mohr and Jessel.

I can identify with David's discomfort at listening to the transsexuals on TV talk shows. It turned me off too, because I figured there was something unhealthy and unbalanced about such persons, and I still don't understand their desire to become celebrities. I knew one woman that became a man after she had two sons, and later became a woman again. She told her story on national TV. But I have gained tolerance for those individuals whose sexual orientation does not match their sexual organs because of my close contact with Danielle. She does not want to be given attention because she is a transsexual. She is a girl and has always been a girl and doesn't want people to think about anything else.

What I think is commendable is that Evelyn immediately sought professional advice on how to assist Danielle to make the transition in the way that was best for her. This led to psychological testing, electrolysis, and hormone therapy - treatments which were uncomfortable and sometimes painful for Danielle. The fact that her brothers, cousins, aunts and uncles on both sides of her family were supportive, with one or two exceptions, is also commendable. Some who have had qualms about getting acquainted with Danielle have had their doubts immediately swept away when they meet the beautiful, vivacious, out-going young lady. Even though I too, understood the situation and knew it was right for Danielle, I have had a real problem with the pronouns - he, she, him, her - but I am getting better at it. I am so pleased to see her blossom scholastically and socially, and her excitement about life is contagious. She has courageously faced the necessary difficulties, and recognizes that the road ahead won't be easy, but she is up to it. Life sometimes uses strange ways to teach us tolerance and understanding of persons who have problems different from our own. How fortunate we are to be able to learn this lesson from Danielle.

III.

Dear Family,

Hello, My name is Danielle. I thought it was time I made an introduction to the family since I am a recent addition to it. It has taken be a long time to decide to introduce myself and am happy that I have finally gotten a small grip of my confidence to do so. I have been through many obstacles and challenges these last three years, for that I owe to my soul searching (my happiness).

My mother is (as many know her) "Just Evelyn". Evelyn who I love, cherish and give thanks for giving me life and happiness. She is a very courageous women, hard worker, and one who has the biggest heart not fully seen by everyone but when seen is never ending. Through hard times and good my mother has raised three children: although she may deny this honorable task, her children know the truth.

I was born December 30, 1978. Since then I have lived two lives that are completely different from each other. At the present I am eighteen years old and very happy to be myself. I will be entering my senior year this fall; I am looking forward to it. I am living in Flagstaff, Arizona, a small town close to the Grand Canyon. Flagstaff is a very beautiful town with mountains surrounding it. It also has many trees. I have made good friends since I have moved to this small town: friendships that are often hard to find and I am glad for them for they have helped me to understand myself and other people. I cannot say how happy I am for some times it hurts and is hard to explain, but I know it is a good feeling, that I have waited so long for, and I know it will not go away.

As most of my family knows and for those who do not, I am a female now but I was born genetically a male. At the age of fifteen I told my mother that I was unhappy being a male and that I wished I could be a woman since I always felt like a women inside me. My, mother was very shocked since she thought I would grow up to be gay. The way I saw it was: I thought as myself being a women and liking a man and the man liking me for being a women so I did not feel gay. After I had told her it was like a wall between us had been torn down. We became one that night as daughter and mother. My mother knew that I was going to need her more than ever, she was also going to need me for support. Together my mother and I could do everything that we wished and we were not going to back down.

I dressed up as a girl the day after I told my mother about me really being a girl. My mother helped me get dressed up for the first time, she didn't say it but I could tell she really enjoyed it. My mother as a little girl I think never blossomed because she had many restrictions. So my mother lived out her childhood by watching me blossom into a very happy girl. When the shock had gone away from telling her, my mother began a mission to find out as much information as possible since I was anxious to start my new life. We soon found out that my complete transformation was going to take awhile. I had to first live full time as a women for one year and have two counselors evaluate me before I could have sex reassignment surgery (a sex change) I also had to change schools so that I could start as a girl since at the school I was at, they knew me as a boy. I was starting a new life. Those few weeks after I told my mother we were creating a new person. A girl was being born. Her name is Danielle.

On the date of June 27, 1996 I had my sex reassignment surgery in Neenah, Wisconsin. My mother was very helpful to me during it and I could not have done it without her. Clela Fuller, my grandmother, dropped in right after my surgery, which made me very happy that I had support from family. I was in the hospital nine days. On the seventh day, I got up from bed rest. The surgery turned out to be less painful than I had originally thought. A year has passed since then and I've just gone through breast augmentation, which was very painful, but once again my mother was there to make it as easy as possible on me. Now that I have done everything surgery-wise, I am having fun blossoming into who I was always supposed to be. I am dating guys and just having a great time. If only you could all see my happiness.

I will always love everyone.

Danielle

PART V.....EPILOGUE

Fifteen years have passed now for Danielle, as many years living as a female as she lived trying to be a boy. She is a beautiful young woman. Life has had its ups and downs.

After seven years her father finally began warming up to her and now is very supportive and accepting. She never gave up on him and kept showing up at family gatherings.

Danielle lives in Arizona, works as a waitress at a fun restaurant and continues to take college classes part time. Her goals change from time to time. She has thought about being a counselor, a nurse, or a police person. She gets involved in local and national politics and joins demonstrations in her home town. She is part of the transgender activist efforts off and on. She has written various papers for school using transgender as a subject. The subject is new and interesting and something that she knows about. When I ask her if she outed herself, she tells me that she outed me by telling the class that I do electrolysis and have many transgender clients that she has gotten to know. Sometimes she just wants to blend in and not be special.

She has dated various men, but not found one that she wants to live with full time yet. She did have a live-in guy for a while. He really loved her and was very good to her. They are still friends, but he was participating in some dangerous activities so she moved on. Maybe there is someone for her in the future. For the time being, she is becoming more comfortable with being single. The dilemma never goes away, when do you tell a new friend? I see her using more common sense when it comes to relationships than most people I know.

Being transgender does not go away. Recently Danielle needed an x-ray, and the medical clinic asked several times if she was pregnant. She told them no and that she was transsexual. They wanted to know if she was on birth control pills or did she have a hysterectomy? She assured them that those were not options for her. Then the director of the clinic asked her nicely if she could provide proof of being transsexual. They wanted to cover their liabilities, and maybe they just did not believe her. So if she wants to go stealth for medical care, she has to be prepared to have a pregnancy test now and then. They have worked with her trying to stabilize her hormones at the lowest dose that will still be effective. She did find a good counselor who helped her get off of Prozac and still function. She did not like feeling like a "zombie" on Prozac and thought that it might be lessening her libido.

David, her older brother, lives in Idaho. He is married and helped raise his three stepchildren. He did not feel the need to have children of his own. He is a good community person and mentors teens that need help getting headed in the right direction. He and his wife enjoy motorcycle riding. He works in the computer industry, and one of his co-workers transitioned on the job. What a small world.

Ben, the younger brother, is also married and they now have 3 little boys. They live in Colorado and are very busy with the children.

I met a wonderful person and we have been married for almost 6 years. We moved to Colorado to be near the grandchildren. My spouse is part of the transgender community, so is supportive and understanding and helps with activist efforts. We were really meant to be together. I don't know how I managed my life for so many years by myself.

I retired from electrolysis after 10 years. I loved the work and being part of the transgender community, but inflicting pain on others became harder and harder on my soul. Another person wanted to take over the support group that I had started, and it died slowly and painfully. As with many groups, a few sad people felt the need to tear it apart. I tried to be part of several other support organizations, but found so much infighting and power/ego problems that I had to resign.

I have also found many wonderful activists who have become friends as we try to change the world. I finally became part of a group that is advocating and educating for gender variant children. TransYouth Family Advocates (TYFA) is doing wonderful things. I would have loved to have the information that they provide on that night long ago when my child came out to me. Now on one web page a parent can find the information that it took me months to figure out by myself.

The computer has really made a difference in all aspects of our lives. But there is still so much work to be done to make the world a safe place for gender variant children. In 15 years we have come a long way, and yet we are still in the same place. The diagnosis Gender Identity Disorder still gives the impression that this is a mental problem, and most counselors are still not educated enough to be helpful, and still have a conflict of interest when counseling families of gender variant children.

Medical professionals for the younger gender variant people are still rare and medical expenses not covered by most insurance. Schools are still very uptight about how to accommodate these children. More colleges are supportive about the needs of young adults in this situation, but high schools, middle schools, and elementary schools still need education. There have been several examples where one teacher or principal has been supportive, but when the lawyers, social workers, and teachers unions find out, the good intentions are squashed. It is amazing how many adults are intimidated by a 6 yr. old gender variant child.

The media has done some good shows on transgender people, young and old. More and more people have at least been exposed to the facts. There is still too much sensationalizing involved. I wonder if it is about ratings or education and what is the cost to the families involved.

I have hope for the future as I learn of more and more gender variant children who are supported and celebrated by a circle of people who love them.

PART VI.......RESOURCES

ADVICE TO TEENS

If you are a youth questioning your gender identity, you are not alone. There are many more like you than most people realize. There are other teens that feel the same way that you do. Your best source of information is the Internet, or your local gay and lesbian center.

You can succeed and become who you need to be. It is not easy or cheap. You are very fortunate if you have a supportive family. I would suggest that you make at least one attempt to let your family know. I would have been able to start helping my child so much sooner if she would have told me sooner. Leave a book or pamphlet laying around by accident that addresses gender issues. Talk about a "friend" wanting to be a different gender than they appear or bring up the subject with your mother. If she freaks, then back off. Tell her you were just kidding, or under stress or going crazy. Then suggest that maybe you need counseling and see what happens.

At all costs, try not to get kicked out of the house. Stay in school, you are going to need a really good job to pay the bills involved in becoming comfortable with your gender. You can do it by yourself, but it takes longer and you may have to put it off until you can support yourself.

There is family you are born with and family you gather as you go along. If your family cannot accept You, don't drag them along behind you for years. It is a great weight on your karma. Take care of yourself, find accepting friends, adopt other people who need family and then maybe someday your family will catch up with you.

You have the right to be the gender that you feel you are inside. You are not hurting anyone else, they are hurting themselves. You are not sinning, you are not crazy. You are not a second-class citizen. You deserve the best, and if no one else will help you, then do it for yourself.

Your sexual orientation is completely separate from your gender identity. Labels don't always work. You can feel attracted to men, or women, or both or neither. Who you are attracted to can change as you figure out who you are. It's OK! There is nothing wrong with you. Accept other people for who they are regardless of gender.

Your transition is your trip at your speed. There are some minimum times prescribed by the Henry Benjamin standards. But if it takes you 2 years to start hormones, or you stay in the androgynous stage for months, it's OK. This is your trip and there are no maps.

Keep living. Don't put life off until you can have surgery. Enjoy the humor in life. Enjoy every day as another day in becoming you.

ADVICE TO PARENTS

After searching for the perfect way to raise a transsexual, I have found that every transsexual has a different set of challenging situations and a different set of solutions. The following points are my personal opinions only and should be added to any other information available and to the parent's own common sense. Demand good care! Do not consider yourself a beggar, a victim, or a second-class citizen. Let your teen set his or her own pace. Discuss options, but let your teen make the decisions about his or her life whenever possible. Keep a sense of humor, and use lots of hugging.

Medical professionals are quick to prescribe anti-depressants, but are not so good at monitoring for signs of trouble. You know your child best; keep a close eye on her or his progress.

WARNING: In 2005, the US Food and Drug Administration issued a warning for the second time that people taking anti-depressant drugs should be monitored closely for signs of worsening depression and suicidal thoughts.

HIGH SCHOOL

Moving to a new neighborhood and a new school during the summer worked really well for us although I know of a few transsexuals who have survived transition at their current school.

Ask the school district about alternative schools, home schooling and alternative PE programs in your area.

Ask the school district if they have a Gay / Lesbian / Bisexual /Transgender student union on any of their school campuses, or if there are any openly gay teachers at any school. These campuses are more likely to be accepting of diversity.

Have your teen decide which bathroom he/she would feel more comfortable using and then encourage him/her to just go ahead and use those facilities. If you let the school administrators make a choice, they may choose something that is not acceptable to you and your teen.

Unless your teen is ready and strong enough to be an activist, the fewer people in the school that know, the better.

COUNSELING

Questions to ask a prospective counselor:

- What educational degrees do you have?
- Are you licensed by the state in which you practice, and licensed by which state agency?
- How many teen transsexual clients do they have? (seeing them on TV talk shows does not count). If they have seen none, or only one, this lets them know that you know that they are not an expert. Since you will be teaching them, maybe you can negotiate a better per hour price. (Don't count on it.).
- Do you know the difference between sex and gender, gender and orientation, crossdressers and transsexuals?
- How do transsexual teen issues differ from those of an adult? (some differences teens must address are problems with school, parents, dating, sexual orientation, peer pressure, self-esteem, while adults face problems with employment, family, marriage, children, finances, learning feminine mannerisms.)
- Do you have a current copy of the Harry Benjamin Standard of Care, do you follow them, and if so, how strictly?
- Do you require psychological testing? Which tests? How much do they cost? Who will administer them? Will the client or parents receive written results?
- What is the minimum number of visits before you will write a surgery referral letter.

- Do you know the side effects of hormones? (Be sure the counselor mentions or knows about the emotional side effects.)
- How do you feel about prescribing Prozac and why?

An experienced counselor should:

- Know at least one endocrinologist.
- Know one transsexual friendly electrologist.
- Know the local support groups.
- Be able to give you names of relevant books on the subject.
- Know the requirements and forms for changing the Drivers license, and Social Security.
- Know contacts in the local school district.

ENDOCRINOLOGIST

Questions to ask:

- How many transsexuals have you treated?
- What do you charge for a new patient physical exam'?
- Do you give a discount for cash payments?
- Is your staff understanding of the issues?
- What laboratory tests do you require and at what intervals?
- Who does your laboratory work, and do you have a financial interest in the lab?
- What is your usual regimen for treating transsexuals?
- Do you use an androgen blocker?
- What are the side effects of hormones, emotional and physical?

- Will you work with us if we want to try different things, such as injections versus oral hormones, or synthetic versus animal origin hormones?
- What happens if hormones are discontinued?
- What hormones do you prescribe post sex reassignment surgery?

ELECTROLYSIS

IT IS AN ART, NOT A SCIENCE. The skills of the practitioner are more important than the method, or the type of machine that they use.

- Electrolysists are required to be licensed in some states, but not in others.
- Costs can range from $25 to $100 per hour. Some offer discount for multiple hours paid in advance. Electrolysis schools are a less expensive option.
- One should begin to see permanent results after 20-25 hours of treatment in one area.
- A full beard may take up to 300 hours of treatment or more.
- Any marks from weekly electrolysis treatments should be gone in two to three days.
- Ask other transsexuals for referrals and look at their skin to see if they have scars or pitting, especially on the upper lip area.
- Shaving is the preferred method to use between electrolysis treatments
- All electrolysists should be using a new disposable needle for each appointment.
- He/she should have and use a sterilizer to sterilize the tweezers after each client.

- Before and after pictures are sometimes used, but taking full nude pictures is not an acceptable practice.
- Laser hair removal has mixed results: it works better on some types of hair, on some people. I personally know people who have had to go back to electrolysis after laser treatment to complete their hair removal. I think there has been much improvement and laser will be the way of the future. For your time, pain and money, the best value is to start with laser and then finish up with electrolysis.
- I am often asked about home electrolysis units but I have had no hands on experience with them. I have seen pictures and read the instructions and seen the scars as a result of infection on one client that had used such a machine. It is very hard to use these units on oneself. They are very slow in comparison to what an electrolysist can do, and the needles that are used repeatedly are less safe than the disposable needles used by electrolysists today. These small machines may be useful if there are only a few hairs that need to be removed.

SURGEONS

Questions to ask the surgeon that is being considered:

- Do you do sex reassignment surgery on teens and how many have you treated?
- Do you require consent for minors from both parents?
- How much does the surgery cost, and what is included? (This and other routine information may be available in a brochure. Transportation costs are in addition to the cost of surgery.)

- Do you require genital area electrolysis? If so, why? What have been the complications that you have seen that were caused when genital electrolysis was not done? What percentage of patients have had complications from hair in the wrong place post surgery.?
- What percentage of your patients need donor skin?
- Are there visible scars after surgery and where are they? Do you have pictures of persons with the post-surgery scars?
- Is the surgery done in one step, or is a second surgery necessary (labiaplasty)?
- Is there a care facility for post surgical patients, or do they go to a motel for a few days?
- What is the dilating schedule after surgery? What kind of dilator do you recommend?
- Do you have a waiting list?

* * * * *

Writing is one of my coping skills. This following piece was written in the middle of the night when I could not sleep due to the anger and frustration with the counseling and medical industry.

THE VULTURES

As luck would have it, a girl child was born in the body of a boy child and no one knew until the child came to the age of 15, when he revealed himself to a loving mother who quickly saw the anguish and dilemma of her son. She had seen his feminine side and the sorrow in his eyes. She went to seek advice from the counselors of the land and found the vultures instead. Although none had dealt with this problem in the bloom of youth, all were ready to charge high prices for their *expertise*. There were rules written by unseen Gods in the sky concerning these matters. One must first consult one of the above- mentioned *"experts"* until they deem the child sane and capable of knowing what he/she feels inside, and only then they allowed to use the magic potion that starts the physical changes from boy to girl.

The administrators of the magic potion also have their rules and practice much poking and bloodletting. Then the child must convince at least two of the above-mentioned *"experts"*, that the child is not crazy, but was simply born with the wrong body parts. The child must continue consulting the vultures that have no experience for at least half a year and the child must live as a girl to match her heart and soul for at least a year before one can progress to the surgeons. Showing wisdom, the child asks why one does not need the advice of two experts before one has children, or gets married as the child sees that many do not realize the problems involved in those decisions. Why must they ask her so many questions when he knows very clearly what she feels inside? Why do they question her intelligence when anyone can clearly see that this boy has become a beautiful girl and only needs help removing the extra parts that are like a tumor to her.

Can they not see that within this one being is such a war, that the battle is often lost to drink, or drugs, or self-destruction. The vultures wait for the dead bodies. How many have they picked clean so there is no money or strength to continue the journey to the surgeons who sculpt the new parts? Along the way are the people who know what God thinks and judge the child as a sinner. There are others who cannot see the goodness in the child and shun her as if she were diseased, or might hurt them in some way. The mother can only hug the child and do her best to pay the prices demanded, but has been given no advice on how to help the child to be happy and whole. She tries to shield the child from the evils of the advisors who question the child's intelligence and sanity, all the while degrading what small self-esteem the mother has been able to muster within her child with her love and encouragement. The vultures ignore her love and understanding of the child; no one asks her opinion about the future of the child, they only ask for money from her. In ancient times such children were considered as the spiritually gifted because they understood both men and women. When and how has it become an indication of insanity?

After passing through the long and narrow valley full of vultures, the child is able to submit her beautiful young body to the knife of the surgeon who does remove the unwanted parts, but in so doing left unsightly scars in other visible areas. The surgeons do much experimenting on the bodies of thankful victims, trying to perfect their art and become the best in the land, but in the meantime making many mistakes. The mother's heart breaks when she sees what has been done, but the child is so thankful to have the right body that allows her to be as one inside and outside, that the scars are a small price. So the mother hugs the child who is now whole and happy and ready to get on with her life, but the shadow of the vultures remain in the mother's heart.

GLOSSARY

This list, compiled from TransYouth Family Advocates, Inc. and various sources, is terminology commonly used when discussing gender variance, expression and identity. We embrace some less common terms because we believe that they more accurately describe the experiences of gender variant youth and their families. These terms are italicized.

Sexual Orientation - A person's romantic, spiritual and emotional attraction to another. Sexual Orientation is often confused with gender identity; however, is related to who you are attracted to, rather than your gender identity. Some common sexual orientations are queer, gay, lesbian, bi-sexual, pan-sexual, and heterosexual.

Gender Identity - The internal sense of masculinity or femininity that a person experiences, not always congruent with biological sex or gender assigned at birth. Gender identity is who you are not who you like.

"Gender Identity Disorder" - "Gender Identity Disorder" is a diagnostic category in the Diagnostic and Statistical Manual of Mental Disorders (DSM-IV), published by the American Psychiatric Association (APA, Revision IV-TR, 2000). In its current form, the diagnosis is controversial among transgender advocates and mental health professionals. TYFA supports reform and rethinking of the diagnosis as it appears in the DSM-IV. For more information, please visit www.gidreform.org

Gender Dysphoria- A persistent distress with one's physical sex characteristics or assigned birth sex role.

Gender Expression- The ways in which a person socially presents themselves to the world through clothing, hairstyles, toys and other preferences. Most people's gender expression is congruent with their physical sex characteristics or birth sex.

Gender Variant- Those whose gender identity or expression differ from expectations for their physical sex characteristics or birth sex.

Affirm- We use the word 'affirm' to acknowledge the gender identity of an individual. It is our position that they are not changing their gender rather we are changing our

125

perceptions based upon what the individual has expressed to us.

Affirmed Female- (mtf or m2f) An individual who was born anatomically male, however, identifies as female.

Affirmed Male- (ftm or f2m) An individual who was born anatomically female, however, identifies as male.

Social Transition- The outward change in appearance and/or presentation that affirmed females and affirmed males may undergo in order to express their gender identity.

Medical Transition- Undergoing medical intervention(s) to alter physical/sexual characteristics of one's body in order to affirm their gender identity.

Tanner Stages- The 5 stages of puberty represented on the Tanner growth chart. These stages are based on the growth of pubic hair in both sexes, the development of the genitalia in boys, and the development of breasts in girls. This is the criteria that endocrinologists use to determine the appropriate intervals for medical intervention with either puberty inhibitors or hormone treatment.

Puberty Inhibitors, GnRh Inhibitors, Puberty Suppressors, Hormone Suppressors, Puberty Blockers- Medications prescribed by an endocrinologist to delay the onset of puberty. The effects of these medications are reversible. These drugs prevent the devastating unwanted secondary sexual characteristics that occur during adolescence for children whose gender identity conflicts with their birth sex.

Hormone Treatment, HRT (Hormone Replacement Therapy)- The introduction of hormones by an endocrinologist or other health care provider to facilitate development of the desired secondary sexual characteristics associated with the gender identity of the

126

individual. Some of the effects of hormone treatment may not be reversible.

Gender Reconstructive Surgery- (SRS or Sexual Reassignment Surgery) Surgical procedure(s) performed on an individual whose gender identity does not match their assigned birth sex.

READING RECOMMENDATIONS

Brown, Mildred and Rounsley, Chloe Ann, *True Selves Understanding Transsexualism for Family, Friends, Coworkers and Helping Professionals*. San Francisco: Jossey-Bass, 1996.

Stringer, JoAnn Altman, *The Transsexual's Survival Guide II: To Transition and Beyond for Family, Friends and Employers*. Creative Design Services, 1992.

Moir, Anne and Jessel, David, *Brain Sex, The Real Difference Between Men and Women*. Dell Pub/Bantam Doubleday, 1992.

Feinberg, Leslie, *Transgender Warriors: Making History from Joan of Arc to RuPaul*. Boston: Beacon Press, 1996

Israel, Bianna and Tarver, D., *Transgender Care: Recommended Guidelines, Practical Information, and Personal Accounts*.Philadelphia: Temple University Press, 1997.

NATIONAL TRANSGENDER ORGANIZATIONS AND RESOURCES

Female to Male International (FTMI)
160 14th St.
San Francisco, CA 94103
(415) 553-5987
http://www.ftmi.org/
Email: info@ftmi.org

GID Reform Advocates
-advocating reform of psychiatric policies that equate gender diversity with mental illness.
http:www.gidreform.org
Email: kelley@gidreform.org

The International Federation for Gender Education (IFGE)
-a source for information, referrals books.
IFGE
PO Box 229
Waltham, MA 02254-0229
(617) 899-2212
http://www.ifge.org/
Email: IFGE@world.std.com

LynnConway.Com
-a multilingual informational and support resource for transgender and transsexual people by Professor Lynn Conway
http://www.lynnconway.com
Email: lynn@ieee.org

National Center for Transgender Equality (NCTE)
1325 Massachusetts Ave., Suite 700
Washington, DC 20005
(202) 903-0112
http://www.nctequality.org/
Email: ncte@nctequality.org

National Transgender Advocacy Coalition (NTAC)
P O Box 76027
Washington, DC 20013
(978) 373-8898
http://ntac.org/
Email: ntac@comcast.net

Parents, Families and Friends of Lesbians and Gays (PFLAG).
1726 M Street, NW, Suite 400
Washington, D.C. 20036
(202) 467-8180
http://www.pflag.org/
Email: info@pflag.org

PFLAG Transgender Network (TNET)
http://www.pflag.org/tnet.html

Transgender Law and Policy Institute
328 Flatbush Avenue, Box 312
Brooklyn, NY 11238
Email: query@transgenderlaw.org

TransYouth Family Advocates (TYFA)
TYFA
PO Box 1471
Holland, Mi. 49422-1471
(888) 462-8932
http://www.imatyfa.org
Email: info@imatyfa.org

Just Evelyn is the original trailblazer for the current movement to support childhood gender transition. Over 15 years ago she began paving the way for those of us who are now advocating on behalf of our gender variant and transgender children. This book provides all readers with insight, but will be particularly poignant for the children and families living the experience today.

Kim Pearson, Executive Director, TransYouth Family Advocates, Inc.

It is not enough to prepare our children for the world, we must prepare the world for our children.

Luis J. Rodriguez

Made in the USA
Lexington, KY
15 June 2010